551.5
Col   Collins young scientist's
          book of cold

SEP 13			
FEB - 7			
FEB 14			
FEB 24			
FEB 25			
MAR 5			
MAY 2 1			

DEMCO

Cold

FIND THE ANSWER . . .

Collins Young Scientist's book of

COLLINS
GLASGOW AND LONDON

First published in this edition 1976
Published by William Collins Sons and Company Limited
Glasgow and London
© 1976 William Collins Sons and Company Limited
Devised and created by Berkeley Publishers Limited

Published in the United States
by Silver Burdett Company,
Morristown, N.J.
Library of Congress Catalog Card
No. 79-65902   ISBN 0-382-06350-3

CONTENTS

INTRODUCTION

Man has been accustomed to cold for many thousands of years. For most of that vast time-span it has been one of his cruellest enemies. Today it can be both an enemy and an ally. It can help us in many of our industrial processes. It has made possible the most delicate and complicated surgery and it has enabled us to receive clear messages from space. Today we have in some measure tamed and harnessed cold to our needs, and yet our inbred fear of it remains. And with reason — for today, scientists are discussing the possibility of a return of the Ice Ages, although it is 12,000 years since the great ice sheets retreated. In a new Ice Age most of civilized Europe and North America would again be covered with ice.

All this makes it important that we should understand the nature of cold — its risks and its benefits. This book tells the story of cold in all its aspects. We see cold in use in our homes, factories and hospitals. We see how it has altered the very shape of our earth — and we learn how this process could be repeated.

The book is one in a series of books for young scientists and for people of all ages who seek to know more about the nature of the world we all share.

ROALD AMUNDSEN *(1872-1928), the Norwegian explorer who discovered the South Pole, beating England's Captain Scott by a month, was born near Oslo. On his dash to the Pole in 1910 with four companions, Amundsen used dogs to pull the sledges. It was this use of dog teams that finally demonstrated their superiority over men as 'hauling' animals. Pulling a sledge in polar conditions is an enormous effort for a man. Amundsen and his party reached the Pole fit and well-fed. Scott's team arrived exhausted and sick. Amundsen's original plan was to try for the North Pole but on leaving Norway he decided to sail south and make for the South Pole instead.*

ROBERT FALCON SCOTT *(1868-1912), the British naval captain who led an expedition to the South Pole and arrived on 17 January, 1912, only to find that Roald Amundsen had beaten him by a month. Scott and his party ran into blizzard conditions on the return journey and suffered from sickness and food shortages. One member of the team, Captain Oates, walked out in a blizzard to his death. He knew that in his weak state he was slowing the party down. The bodies of Scott, E. A. Wilson and Lieutenant H. R. Bowers were later found in their tent along with Scott's diaries, (his records of the journey and the geological specimens which had been collected during the expedition).*

ROBERT EDWIN PEARY *(1856-1920) was an officer in the United States Navy. On 6 April, 1909, Peary, accompanied by his aide Matthew Henson, and four Eskimos, reached the North Pole. Peary's dash to the Pole was the crowning achievement of 23 years of Arctic exploration. His diary of the epic trek records his triumph in these words: 'I had taken thirteen single or six and one half double altitudes of the sun at two different stations in three different directions at four different times . . . at some moment during these marches and countermarches I had passed over or very near the point where North and South and East and West blend into one.'*

The coldest places on earth

Ever since the beginning of history mankind has had to live with low temperatures. For many thousands of years snow and ice have been a part of the human experience. The great ice sheets have advanced and retreated. Even 10,000 years ago they covered most of Europe. Today, when we think of 'cold' we think immediately of the great white wastes of the Arctic and Antarctic and of the North and South Poles. But although it is true that these are the coldest places on our earth it is a mistake to regard them as just white wildernesses. For the cruellest and coldest lands on earth are in fact extremely beautiful and colourful.

One of the men in Captain Scott's heroic journey to the South Pole described the Antarctic as 'seldom white'. Mostly he saw it as cobalt blue and rose shot through with all the shades of blue and mauve. 'Add to this' he wrote, 'the beautiful tints in the sky, the delicate shading on the snow and the deep colours of the open sea with reflections from the ice-foot and the ice cliffs, all brilliant emerald greens, then, indeed, a man may realise how beautiful this world can be – and how clean.'

Certainly these polar lands are clean. So clean that even germs cannot thrive.

An Arctic or Antarctic blizzard is one of the most terrible experiences on earth. Captain Scott, caught in a blizzard on the world's biggest glacier, wrote: 'Great God, this is an awful place.' And one of his men wrote: 'During the blizzard the drift drove at you in such

NORTH
POLE

Route
taken by
Peary

*

SOUTH
POLE

Route
taken by
Amundsen

Route
taken by
Scott

blankets of snow that your person was immediately blotted out, your face covered and your eyes plugged up.' Most of the time the blizzard winds rage at speeds of 90 kph (60 mph) to 110 kph (70 mph). When Peary made his dash to the North Pole in 1909, brandy in a bottle under his layers of deerskin clothing froze solid. Inside the party's snow igloos their breath condensed and froze to their fur hoods. Cheeks and noses had to be carefully thawed out. Even the meat they ate was so frozen that it cut the roofs

and sides of their mouths. Finally, they boiled it in their tea. Dog teams and men vanished in the frozen fog banks of their own breath. Blizzard-blown ice particles bit into the flesh like shrapnel.

Before the age of modern machinery and air transport these lands of the polar regions were the greatest endurance test on earth for the explorer. Yet during the International Geophysical Year in 1957 a station called Amundsen-Scott was established by air at the South Pole itself.

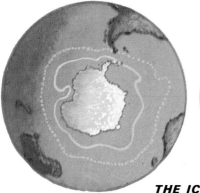
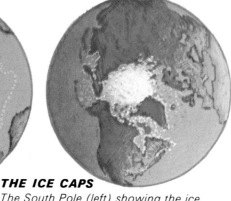

THE ICE CAPS

Summer limit

Winter limit

The South Pole (left) showing the ice cap and summer and winter limits of the pack ice. The Northern ice cap (right) spans the Arctic Ocean, Greenland and Northern Canada and the USSR.

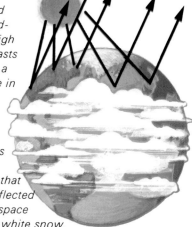

PACK ICE

Summer pack ice in the Antarctic waters. The ice, which stretches far out to sea, is impenetrable after the southern winter.

MIDNIGHT SUN

The Arctic is called the land of the midnight sun, for in high summer daylight lasts for 24 hours. Left: a typical night scene in Iceland in June.

Reflected heat

SOLAR HEAT

is less intense at the Poles than at the equator. It also varies with the earth's tilt, as we show on the far right.

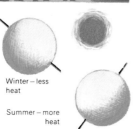

Winter – less heat

Summer – more heat

CLOUDS

There are few clouds at the Poles because of little evaporation. Heat that reaches earth is reflected directly back into space by the expanse of white snow.

Cold and the polar regions

We have already seen that the areas round the North and South Poles are the coldest and most deserted places in the world. The North Pole is ice on top of water – indeed it is literally in the middle of the Arctic Ocean. The northern polar region falls within the Arctic circle at a latitude of $66\frac{1}{2}°$N, while the North Pole itself is found at 90°N. The Antarctic region is geographically described as being beyond $66\frac{1}{2}°$S. Both these polar regions rank as deserts. Any 'rainfall' is almost entirely in the form of snow.

Both the Arctic and Antarctic have seasons. In the Arctic winter, December 22 is the 'shortest' day (actually 24 hours of darkness). But the longest summer day – around June 21 – has 24 hours daylight, which is why the Arctic is named the 'land of the midnight sun'.

The shape of the earth plays a major part in making both the regions so cold. Energy from the sun reaching the polar regions has to spread over a far wider area there than at the equator. This

dilutes both the solar light and heat. The tilt of the earth towards the sun is another reason for the Poles' intense cold. The north polar regions tilt towards the sun in summer and away from it in winter.

The Antarctic receives more solar radiation than the Arctic but is colder because there is a greater north to south air flow and the Arctic Ocean also has a moderating effect on the climate of the North Pole. The floating pack ice of the North Pole is five metres (16 ft) deep on average and the Arctic

POLAR PLANTS
Three flowers that survive the severe cold of the polar regions - gentians, buttercups and calceolarians.

Gentian

Buttercup

Calceolaria

HOUSES IN THE SNOW
Most scientific camps at the South Pole are built underground. Houses and work units are connected by vast tubes cut into the ice.

THE EMPEROR PENGUIN
is one of the few birds which lives at the South Pole all the year. A tall, hefty bird, well insulated with fat, it survives −65°C (−85°F).

LIFE AT THE SOUTH POLE
The freezing temperatures of the South Pole attract few people. Most of the inhabitants are scientists and surveyors.

WEIGHT OF ICE
The Greenland ice cap is more than 3000 metres thick. The vast weight of this ice pushes down the land underneath.

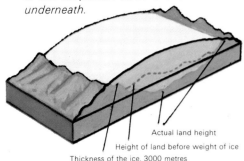

Actual land height

Height of land before weight of ice

Thickness of the ice, 3000 metres

Ocean is about 800 km (500 miles) across. The island of Greenland is completely covered with an ice-cap up to 3000 metres (two miles) deep in places. The Antarctic is covered by a much vaster ice-cap surrounded by huge sheets of ice. Sea ice projects beyond the land ice for about 1250 km (780 miles) to 1450 km (910 miles).

The land under the Antarctic is in two halves – one an archipelago and the other a series of high plateaux separated by lowlands. The ice-cap at the South Pole is 3000 metres (two miles) thick and the

greatest known ice-cap thickness is 5600 metres (three and a half miles).

Average temperatures in the Arctic vary from the pack ice area 0°C (32°F) to −35°C (−31°F) to Central Greenland 15°C to −40°C (59°F to −40°F). The lowest recorded temperature was −68°C (−90°F) in Siberia. Average mean temperature at the South Pole (3000 metres, or two miles, above sea level) is −51°C (−60°F). The coldest places on earth are to be found on the Antarctic Continent, where −88°C (−126°F) has been recorded.

THE YEARS OF ICE
Our chart shows how the Pleistocene Ice Age, which lasted about one million years, is divided. There were three main phases, the lower (the oldest), the middle and the upper. Each phase had periods of intense glaciation (blue), mild glaciation (grey) and non-glaciation (pink). The last retreat of ice began around 8000 BC in the Holocene era. The chart gives the names of the major glaciations and the average age of each intensely cold, cold, and warm period. The Ice Age as compared to the earth's age (4600 million years) is as 3/4 second is to an hour.

GONDWANALAND
About 350 million years ago Australia, South America, Africa, India and Antarctica probably formed one great land mass mostly covered with ice. We call this Gondwanaland and it was centred on today's South Pole. As the earth's crust moved and developed, this mass assumed the form of today's land areas. Our map shows the position of this Continent.

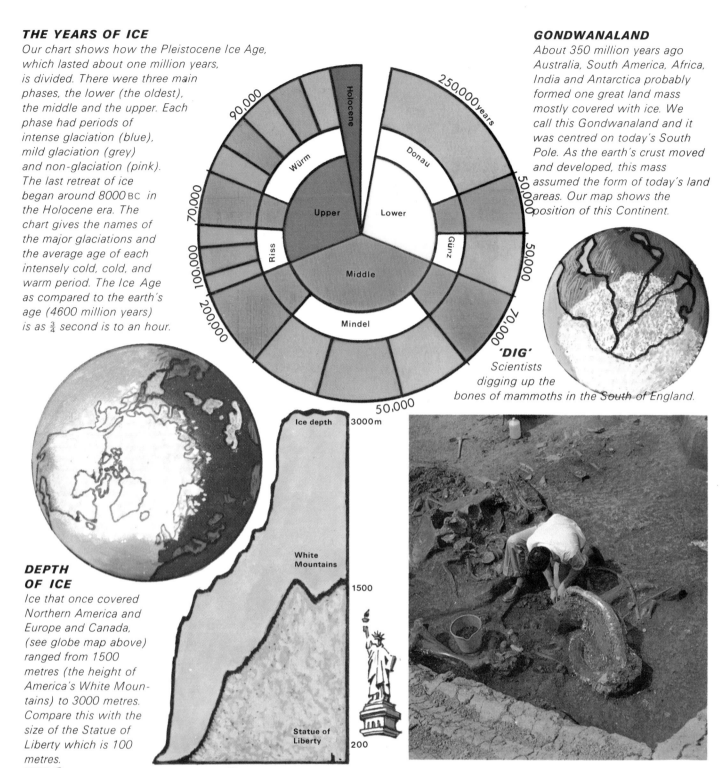

'DIG'
Scientists digging up the bones of mammoths in the South of England.

DEPTH OF ICE
Ice that once covered Northern America and Europe and Canada, (see globe map above) ranged from 1500 metres (the height of America's White Mountains) to 3000 metres. Compare this with the size of the Statue of Liberty which is 100 metres.

The great Ice Ages

Nobody really knows what caused the great Ice Ages although many theories have been put forward. But although we know very little about their origin we do know that during the last 1,750,000 years there have been several long periods during which Northern Europe and the northern parts of North America have been covered with sheets of ice many hundreds of metres thick. Even before that time it is probable that Australia, South America, Africa, India and Antarctica, which then formed one vast land

mass, were mostly covered with ice.

The more recent Ice Ages were during the Pleistocene period and this period has been divided into three 'time zones' – the lower, the middle and the upper. The Holocene period which followed the Pleistocene marked the retreat of the ice northwards about 8000 BC.

In between the various glacial periods, life ebbed and flowed and different species developed and adapted to the changing conditions. Since 6000 BC climatic conditions have been fairly stable but it is

quite possible that we are even now in yet another between-the-Ice-Ages situation, since Ice Ages seem to be a recurring feature of the earth.

During the Ice Ages, temperatures scarcely rose above freezing point and fell to about −50°C or −60°C (−58°F or −76°F). Some hardy plants survived in sheltered areas. Sheets of ice more than 1000 metres (3280 ft) thick covered all but the highest points, such as the Pennines in England and the Urals and Carpathians in Europe. Pollen from plants growing in these areas

RHINOCEROS
This animal - a woolly rhinoceros - flourished during the great ages of ice. Its thick pelt gave it good protection from the intense cold.

ICE AGE MAMMOTH
This perfectly preserved mammoth was excavated in 1860 from the ice in Siberia. During the Ice Ages, when temperatures rarely rose above 0°C, the large woolly mammoths, musk oxen and reindeer were the only animals to brave the ice sheets. It is believed that the mammoths were decimated by man during the middle to last stages of the Ice Ages.

sometimes became frozen in the soil. It is from these survivals we can build up a rough picture of the vegetation of those times.

In America the ice sheet covered Canada and the northern part of the United States, from the Atlantic to the Rockies and as far south as New York City, Cincinnati, Ohio, Kansas City and Pierre (South Dakota). In New Hampshire it was higher than the White Mountains (1500 metres or 5000 ft) and was probably double that in many areas.

The Ice Ages caused vast changes

ENTER MAN
The estimated time and temperatures of the glacial and interglacial phases. Modern man (Homo sapiens) appeared in the Riss Würm interglacial.

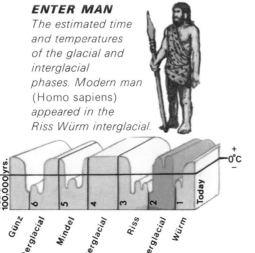

Scale 100,000 yrs.

Günz · interglacial · Mindel · interglacial · Riss · interglacial · Würm · Today

in the formation of the land. The water that formed the ice sheets came from the seas which fell in depth by more than 100 metres (330 ft). Then, as the ice melted, glaciers cut huge fiords and chasms in the earth.

During one period between two Ice Ages the climate in what is now Southern England became almost tropical. The fossilized remains of elephants, rhinoceroses, deer, giant tigers and semi-tropical plants have been found under today's Trafalgar Square, London.

GLACIER FORMATIONS

Glaciers begin at the top of a mountain, above the snow line, where the snow fall is greater than the rate of melting. The snow compacts into an ice pack, becoming thicker and thicker until it may be as deep as 300 metres (1000 ft). The weight of the ice and the force of gravity make the ice flow down the mountain like treacle. This huge mass of moving ice has an abrasive effect on the mountain and cuts out deep valleys and ravines.

CREVASSES

Huge crevasses are often formed when glaciers curve round corners. These cracks in the ice can be as deep as 14 metres (46 ft) and are often 3 metres (10 ft) wide.

A 'SNOUT'

As a glacier flows into a valley, where the temperature is higher, the ice begins to melt. Often this happens as soon as it enters the valley. The end of a glacier is called a 'snout' (see picture below).

A GREAT GLACIER

A magnificent example of a landscape carved by ice - in Alberta, Canada, the great Athabaska Glacier (above) splinters a pathway through the mountain rocks. This is one of North America's most accessible glaciers. The great glaciers of the world are constantly on the move and they exert a crushing force on objects in their path. During a particularly cold spell towards the end of the 16th century, the Alpine glaciers were very active. Small settlements were buried beneath the glacier's slow, ruthless advance. Top soil was stripped away, and even when the glaciers retreated many years elapsed before the soil could be cultivated. Between 1600 and 1940 more than a dozen Alpine glacier advances and retreats were recorded.

Rivers of ice

Glaciers consist of vast masses of ice and snow packed very tightly together. They form in high mountains and in the polar regions. They are really a sort of moving ice mountain and when they move they exert tremendous pressure upon the rocks below, carving huge valleys out of mountain-sides and sometimes forming the basins for great lakes. A glacier's rate of movement depends on the climate and can vary from about one metre to 50 metres (164 ft) a year.

Glaciers start to build up in high regions where the snowfall is greater than the rate of melting and evaporation. A glacier is rather like a sandwich made up of thick layers of snow and thin layers of dust and debris blown on to the snow's surface in the warmer months.

When the snow falls on to the collecting area it is soft and porous since it is made up of ice crystals which have large air spaces between them. Gradually this snow settles and becomes greenish or bluish and transparent.

The pull of gravity and the slip-ping and bending forces within the glacier make the mass of ice gathering in the collecting basin move gradually down the mountain slope. At the lower end of the glacier there is a balance between the ice moving downwards and the melting rate. Melt waters emerge from the tongue, or snout, of the glacier.

Ice cracks when it is not elastic enough to slip smoothly over obstacles on its downward flow. Cracks, or crevasses as they are sometimes called, can be deep. As recently as about 12,000 years ago,

CORRIES

Not all glaciers are formed from the build-up of ice on a mountain top. Sometimes they begin in the hollow of a mountainside where the ice gradually scoops and plucks the rock farther and farther back into the side of the mountain. When the ice melts a hollow is exposed. This is called a corrie and the resulting lake is known as a tarn. Corries are also called cirques. The illustrations below show how the corrie begins and what it looks like eventually, with its tarn.

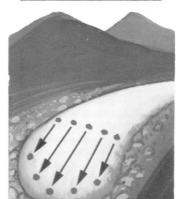

ICE FAN

Sometimes in very cold places like Antarctica and Greenland, the glacier snout reaches the plains without melting and spreads like a giant fan.

GLACIAL FLOW

Not all parts of a glacier move at the same speed. For example, research has demonstrated that the centre of the glacier moves at a faster rate than the sides. This difference in the rate of flow is due to the fact that the ice at the sides of the glacier is slowed down by friction from the surrounding valley walls.

ICEBERGS

break off the polar ice shelf. Eight ninths of their bulk is below water.

during the last great Ice Age, mammoths roaming over the wastes of what is now Russia slipped into these glacier crevasses.

There are several main types of glacier and these are named after the area in which they most commonly occur. Cirque glaciers are common in the Pyrenees and are small ones with hardly any tongue or snout. A valley or Alpine glacier stretches for a long distance down a valley. Alaskan glaciers have a very great depth above which only the peaks of mountains and their higher ridges protrude.

When glaciers retreat or melt away, as they did when the various Ice Ages ended, they left behind them moraines, huge mounds of rubble and boulders. In the Italian Alps, north west of the city of Turin, there is a ridge of these glacial mounds or moraines at the entrance to the Valle d'Aosta. This ridge rises almost 400 metres (1300 ft) from its base.

The rich agricultural soil in the South Midlands area of England was produced by glacial deposits.

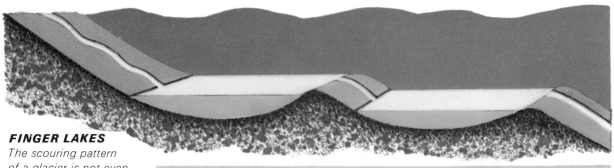

FINGER LAKES

The scouring pattern of a glacier is not even. The valleys can be much wider and deeper in some areas than others. Finger lakes were gouged out of the valley floor by the ice. They are usually about 1·6 kilometres (a mile) in length but can be longer. The melt waters of the glacier then filled the hollows. The drawing above shows a cross-section of Windermere, the largest finger lake in England. It consists of two eight-kilometre (five-mile) rock hollows separated by a rock barrier. This barrier nearly cuts the lake in half. (Right) rocks smoothed by the flow of ice on the glacial bed.

GLACIER TIP

Coniston Old Man in the English Lake District was once the tip of a glacier. That is, a glacier at one time began on top of this mountain. As the ice punched its way down, deep ravines were sculpted out of the sides of the mountain. On the right we show how some moraines were formed by the glaciers. There is a large moraine ridge at Valle d'Aosta, Italy.

Ice and the landscape

At the height of the great Ice Ages 28 per cent of our land surface was ice-covered. Today about 16,400,000 square kilometres (6,500,000 square miles) or some 10·4 per cent of the land surface is under ice and permanently glaciated.

The largest single glacier in the world is probably the Lambert glacier in the Australian Antarctic territory. This vast glacier is 64 km (40 miles) wide in places and with the Fisher limb is about 514 km (320 miles) long.

The great glaciers of the Ice Ages have left their mark all over the world. The Great Lakes in Canada – huge inland seas – were formed by glaciers scouring the plains. The 10,000 lakes of Minnesota and the irregular geographical features of Canada and much of North and South Dakota, Wisconsin and Michigan are due to the action of huge glaciers.

The fiords of Norway, Greenland, Alaska and Chile and parts of New Zealand were carved out from already existing valleys by the relentless movement of the glaciers.

Mountains in places such as Hawaii – now famed for its warm and sunny climate – New Guinea, and Japan, show the tell-tale marks of the ancient glaciers.

The very fertile soils often found in these areas were, in fact, formed from loess, a silt picked up by the powerful winds and spread over great areas, in places to a depth of fifteen metres (50 ft). It is no exaggeration to say that the earth we know today and much of its dramatic scenery, was sculpted out by the action of the ancient glaciers.

MATTERHORN *During the Ice Ages, the Matterhorn in Switzerland was almost entirely eroded by glaciers.*

HANGING VALLEYS

Hanging valleys are the result of two glaciers, one higher than the other. The lower glacier contained more ice and so dug out a deeper path for itself. The higher floor is called the hanging valley and the two are usually connected today by a waterfall.

U-SHAPED VALLEYS

The valleys into which the glaciers flowed were once V-shaped (right) but the ice bulk carved away the steep sides (left). The V became U-shaped and rivers now occupy these valleys.

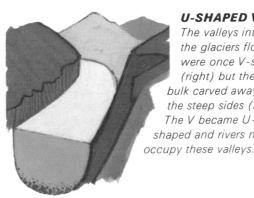

Ice Ages are simply convenient descriptions for several very cold spells, each spell lasting thousands of years. The last main Ice Age – known as the Würm glaciation – had several very cold periods interspersed with 'warmer' periods. The diagram on page 10 shows how these phases were divided. It is difficult to be certain about such remote dates but we show the generally accepted rough divisions.

During the last Ice Age some plant life did survive on the frozen steppes and wastelands, although these plants do not now have their exact modern likeness. But in the Ukraine, for example, even in this last Ice Age the very short summers provided food for grazing animals. Mammoths were hunted by men, their huge bones formed the framework for tent shelters, and their skins were used as a covering for the shelter. These shelters were heated, as the charcoal remains of fires indicate. Simple tools fashioned from animal bones were also used – some of them with quite recognizably modern shapes. Even bone needles have been found at these Ice Age dwelling sites.

TABLE ICEBERGS
Tabular Antarctic icebergs (right) can be as long as 220 km (140 miles) and as high as 70 metres (230 ft). They break off the floating ice shelf and are carried north by the cold polar currents. The inset map shows their maximum range. Some of them drift as far north as Australia before they eventually melt away.

MEETING POINT
In 1922 the US coastguard boat Tampa (below) registered a temperature of 1°C (34°F) at bow and 13°C (55°F) at stern when in the North Atlantic, where the cold Labrador current meets the warm Gulf Stream. This shows how sharply the temperature of the currents can vary.

AN ICEBERG'S PATH
Icebergs leave the Arctic ocean via Davis Strait, between Greenland and Newfoundland. They are carried by the cold Labrador current but melt as they reach the warm Gulf Stream.

Cold Labrador current

Warm Gulf Stream

FOG BANKS
One of the results of the mixture of warm and cold sea currents is the fog (left) produced at their meeting point. The Newfoundland banks are covered with fog for forty per cent of the year. This makes navigation difficult.

POLAR DRIFTS
The Humboldt current from the South Pole is rich in sea food. This makes the Chilean coast one of the world's best fishing grounds. The West Australian current, the Falkland current off eastern South America and the Benguela current off Western Africa (see map) are also cold, food-rich streams from the Antarctic.

The cold sea currents

Ever since man first sailed westwards from Europe, he has found icebergs a problem. Leif Erikson, the Viking navigator, met them on his travels to the northeast coast of America. And even today, although radar has helped to prevent major disasters, icebergs are still a hazard to shipping.

Icebergs calve, or break off, from the glaciers of the Arctic and the Antarctic. In the northern hemisphere they are more numerous in the spring and early summer. Most icebergs leave the Arctic by the Davis Strait between Greenland and Newfoundland. These icebergs have a longer life span than icebergs using other exit routes. This is because there is a strong cold water current moving southwards through these straits. This is called the Labrador current and its temperature is lower than that of the water in the North Atlantic. This current meets a northerly branch of the warm Gulf Stream. The boundary line between these water currents is very clearly defined. There may be a difference of 10°C within a space of 20 km (12·5 miles). In 1922 an American coastguard frigate recorded a temperature of 1°C (34°F) at her bows and 13°C (55°F) at her stern.

The notorious fogs that frequently surround the Newfoundland banks are caused by this dramatic meeting of cold and warm water currents.

Southern icebergs are often larger than their Arctic counterparts. They can be as long as 150 km (93 miles). This is because on the Southern continent large areas of ice

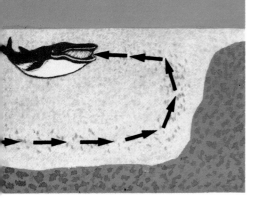

UPWELLING
Antarctic water spreading north returns as 'deep water' and is forced to rise when it reaches the ice shelf, carrying marine debris with it.

COLD SEA FISH
The world map (below) shows the cold ocean currents and the fish that live in them. These fish include the Atlantic herring and cod which are found in the icy waters off Greenland and Iceland, the Arctic char which lives in the Arctic Ocean and the cold seas near Japan, Alaska and Labrador, and the halibut which thrives in sub-arctic waters. The northern pike, like the rockfish, is seen in the cold waters near Alaska. The pike is also seen near Europe and Asia. The coloured dots key the fish to the map.

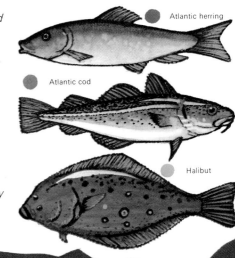

Atlantic herring

Atlantic cod

Halibut

Arctic char

Sperm whales (above) and baleen whales can be found in most of the earth's oceans, including the Polar Seas.

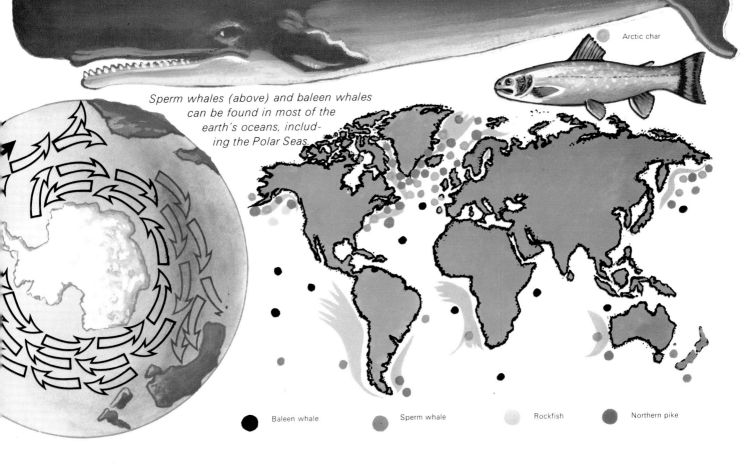

Baleen whale   Sperm whale   Rockfish   Northern pike

shelf break off as tabular icebergs. The icebergs also last longer because the Antarctic is completely surrounded by sea and there are many cold currents drifting northwards to South America, South Africa and Australia.

Some of the richest fishing grounds in the world are in seas fed by the cold currents from the polar regions. The cold Arctic current sweeping through the fishing grounds off Japan is called the Oya Shio, while the Humboldt or Peru current from Antarctica makes the

WHALE DIET
The sperm whale (top) lives on a diet of small fish. The fin whale (below) lives on plankton.

fishing off Chile among the world's best. These cold currents abound in rich minerals, plankton and other marine life. The whales of the Southern Ocean depend upon this cold sea food. The biggest whale – the blue whale – can grow to a length of more than 30 metres (100 ft) and can weigh more than 100 tonnes (99 tons).

Both the Arctic and Antarctic produce very cold water (about −1·4°C or 29°F), which sinks to the bottom of the sea, then moves slowly along the ocean floor.

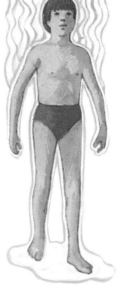

SWIMMING

Evaporation is one of the main ways of losing heat. We soon feel chilled if we stand about after swimming since heat is lost as the water evaporates from our body.

SKIN

Nerve endings cause our blood vessels to constrict when our skin feels cold - see diagram below.

SOIL CREEP

Southern valley slopes can appear step-like. This is soil creep, due to the expansion of freezing water breaking up soil particles (below). Soil creep can tilt poles and trees. Rocks (above) split from a cliff due to water freezing and thawing.

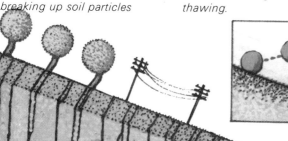

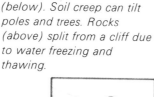

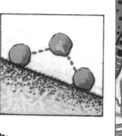

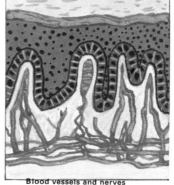

Surface skin and cell layers

Blood vessels and nerves

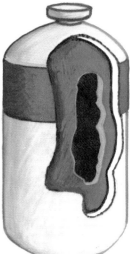

The effects of cold

It is much more difficult to make things cold than to make them hot. This is because it is easier to give a substance more energy than to remove energy. All substances are made up of atoms, usually grouped together into molecules. These molecules are always moving and the more energy they possess the faster they move and so, of course, the hotter they become. All warm objects eventually cool down from loss of heat but they do not cool below the temperature of their environment.

Cooling a substance to very low temperatures can change its qualities considerably. For instance, oxygen and nitrogen in liquid form are very cold ($-200°C$ or $-328°F$). If you put your hand into these liquids it would be very severely burned. If a spongy rubber is immersed in liquid oxygen for several minutes it becomes very hard and brittle – so brittle that if you drop it from a height of even 50 or 60 cm (20 to 24 inches) it will shatter into a great number of tiny pieces.

Water is also changed by cooling.

As it cools it becomes more dense – that is to say it weighs more – until it reaches $4°C$ ($39°F$), when it becomes less dense. Water at $4°C$ is always present in larger pools and lakes because its density makes it sink to the bottom, even though colder water above it might freeze. Because water is a poor conductor of heat the water at the bottom stays at about $4°C$ during the whole winter. That is why fish can survive in frozen pools.

Ice is less dense than water, which is why it floats. It is less

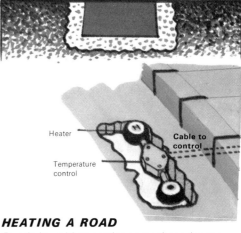

HEATING A ROAD

Roads in cold countries sometimes have a heating system buried beneath the surface. This is switched on when there is a danger of severe ice or snow and is very effective, as our picture shows. The diagram above shows a cross-section of a heating unit in position. Some outside sports grounds have a similar anti-freeze system.

PONDS IN WINTER

Cooling water becomes more dense until it reaches 4°C (39°F) when it becomes less dense. Water at 4°C is always present at the bottom of ponds, which is why fish survive in the pond although the surface freezes.

LIQUID OXYGEN

At −190°C (−310°F) liquid oxygen is very cold. It is stored in metal containers which do not easily expand or contract. The container at left consists of two metal layers divided by a vacuum. The inner layer is of a special stainless steel and the outer layer is of carbon steel, blasted with zinc.

BOTTLES AND PIPES

When water freezes into ice it expands. This is why pipes crack when their contents freeze. On cold days frozen milk sometimes expands out of the bottle (far left). But when a liquid freezes in a glass jar with a screwtop lid, the glass cracks. There is no room for expansion.

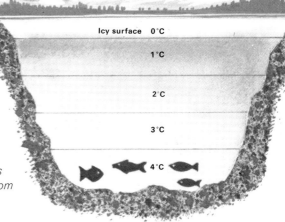

dense because it expands when it freezes. This is why pipes and bottles burst when their contents freeze. The vast icebergs we have already discussed only show about one ninth of their volume above the sea. Since ice is about eight ninths as dense as sea water, this means that an iceberg 50 metres (55 yds) high is also about 400 metres (440 yds) deep.

The freezing of water on soil surfaces – as on hillsides – can cause the soil to crumble. Sometimes this freezing soil can produce

CLOCKS

Pendulums on clocks contract with cold. This is corrected by an adjustable nut.

a terraced effect of ridges. This breaking up of the soil particles is due to the expansion of water as it freezes and is known as 'soil creep'.

Constructional engineers have to take into account the effects of cold and freezing just as much as the effects of heat. Exposed roads and bridges often incorporate a heating 'blanket' a few centimetres below the surface. This is switched on when frost or ice threaten.

Man reacts to the cold by turning blue. Blood vessels contract to save loss of heat.

SNOW AND HAIL
Hailstones can be bigger than matchboxes. They are frozen rain drops and are often accompanied by thunder storms. The beautiful crystals below are snowflakes, enlarged.

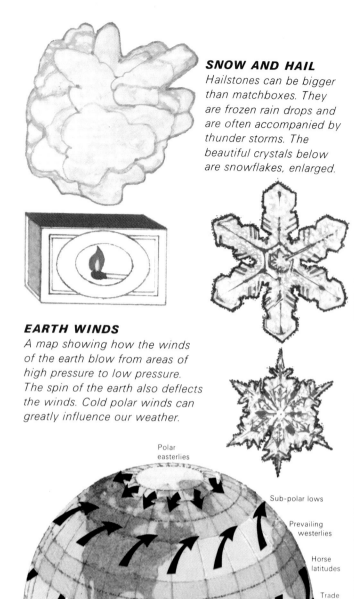

EARTH WINDS
A map showing how the winds of the earth blow from areas of high pressure to low pressure. The spin of the earth also deflects the winds. Cold polar winds can greatly influence our weather.

Polar easterlies

Sub-polar lows

Prevailing westerlies

Horse latitudes

Trade winds

Doldrums

Trade winds

Horse latitudes

Prevailing westerlies

Cold in the air

Between 1884 and 1893 a group of Scottish meteorologists decided to take it in turns to live on Ben Nevis, the highest mountain in Britain, to discover the relationship between cold and altitude, or height. They lived at an altitude of 1322 metres (4400 ft) and the lowest temperature recorded was −17°C (1·4°F), which was not out of the ordinary. But they did discover that the average temperature at the summit was 8·7°C lower than at Fort William which was 1270 metres (4100 ft) below their measuring

point. This meant that the temperature became about 1°C lower for every 146 metres (480 ft) of height.

In 1862, James Glaisher, a well-known meteorologist, made an ascent in an open basket slung beneath a balloon. Not realizing that the air would grow colder as he ascended he wore only a jacket and was unconscious from the cold when the balloon landed. The minimum temperature thermometer read −84°C (−119°F), which corresponds to a height of 11,100 metres

(7 miles). At this altitude there is less air than at the earth's surface.

The earth's atmosphere consists of several layers and all of these layers have different characteristics. The layer of atmosphere in which we live is called the troposphere. In this level of atmosphere the temperature gets colder the higher up we go. Then comes the tropopause, a layer which separates our earth atmosphere from the stratosphere. In the stratosphere the temperature begins to rise again due to the absorption of ultra

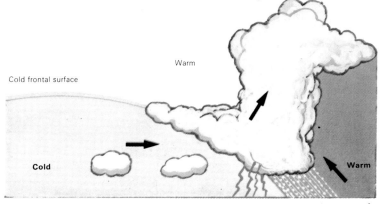

COLD FRONT

When a mass of cold air meets a mass of warm air the warm air rises and if it rises rapidly the result is a billowing cloud often accompanied by rain, thunder and lightning. We show a diagram of this clash of air fronts (above). Cold air has been caught up to the south of this former hurricane (left) as it moves out of hurricane latitudes.

ALTITUDE

James Glaisher's 1862 ascent in an open-basket balloon reads like a Jules Verne story. The intrepid Glaisher did not realize that the higher he went the cooler it would become. He and his friend Coxwell suffered severe frostbite when the temperature plunged to −84°C or −119°F at a height of 11,000 metres (7 miles). They took no precautions against the cold. Glaisher had not realized that for every 1500 metres (5000 ft) of height there is a temperature drop of 8°C. Our illustration (below) shows the effect of this measured against Everest, which at 8537 metres (29,028 ft) is the world's highest mountain.

ATMOSPHERE

For the temperature of different layers read along the red graph. Below: A weather balloon, with its instrument box.

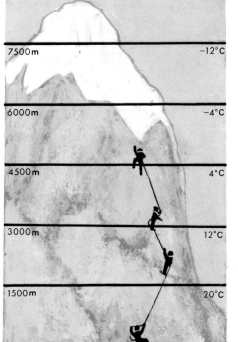

9000m	−20°C
7500m	−12°C
6000m	−4°C
4500m	4°C
3000m	12°C
1500m	20°C
	28°C

violet rays from the sun. Above the stratosphere we have a layer called the mesosphere in which the temperature again decreases with height up to about 80 km (50 miles). Above this layer, in the thermosphere, temperatures again increase dramatically because of the short-wave radiation from the sun.

There are winds at all these levels in the atmosphere.

In the summer, the winds coming from the North Pole are called the polar easterlies and have little effect on British, American and Central European weather. In the winter this direction changes to northerly, and much colder temperatures result. If the winds cross over land masses – for example, Scandinavia or Canada – they become colder and drier and bring quite severe weather conditions. These winds are called polar continental winds. Polar winds blowing south-eastwards over the sea (maritime winds) usually bring brighter, showery weather, while cold air moving due south brings cold conditions with 'biting' winds.

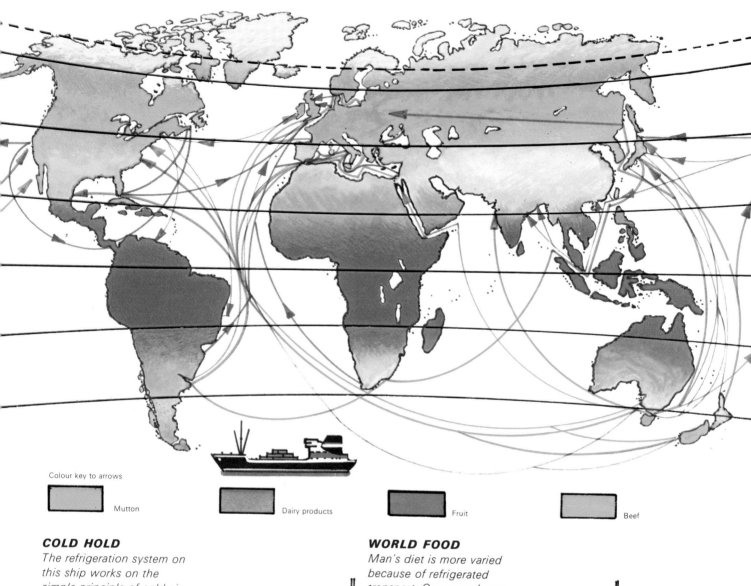

Colour key to arrows

Mutton   Dairy products   Fruit   Beef

COLD HOLD

The refrigeration system on this ship works on the simple principle of cold air circulation. The cold air is pumped through the storage holds from a refrigeration unit. The air is changed constantly and is kept circulating in the cargo holds at a fixed temperature. The system makes possible a hundred air changes every hour and also enables perishable foods to be transported.

WORLD FOOD

Man's diet is more varied because of refrigerated transport. Our map shows how foodstuffs can now be moved round the world.

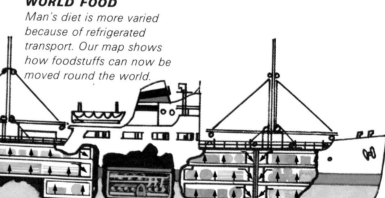

↑ Cold air

Refrigeration plant

Uses of cold

The building of refrigerated ships towards the end of the last century completely changed the trading pattern of the world. Meat, which could now be frozen and preserved during transport, became the major export of New Zealand, Australia and Argentina. But it was not until the 1930s that the domestic refrigerator appeared in our homes and greatly changed our food buying habits. In more recent years the deep freeze unit has again enlarged food storage possibilities.

When a liquid is changed to its gaseous form it absorbs heat since the liquid molecules have to be speeded up to allow them to become gaseous. The heat needed to do this is taken from the liquid's container or its surroundings. This is the way refrigerators work.

Refrigerators were originally used to make ice, which was then used to keep perishable foods fresh. The greatest use of refrigeration is in the preservation of foods, for cold slows down or even prevents the development and activity of the micro-organisms which make food

GREEN FRUIT

Many fruits are picked in an unripe state and kept in cold store. They are then gradually ripened as needed.

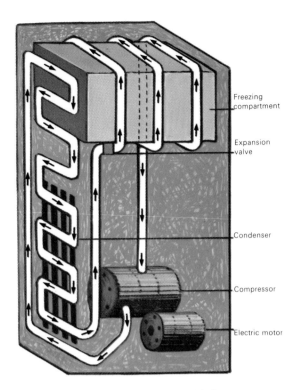

Freezing compartment

Expansion valve

Condenser

Compressor

Electric motor

HOUSEHOLD REFRIGERATORS

In a household refrigerator the refrigerant is compressed into a liquid. It passes through the condenser and then through a valve into a low pressure chamber. In so doing it evaporates and takes heat from inside the freezer.

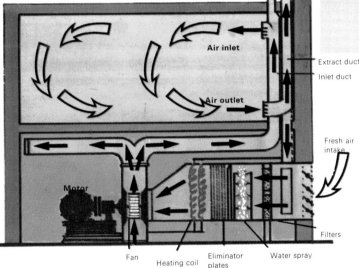

Air inlet

Air outlet

Extract duct

Inlet duct

Fresh air intake

Motor

Fan

Heating coil

Eliminator plates

Water spray

Filters

Refrigeration engine room

Ice rink

AIR CONDITIONING

Air conditioning systems for large buildings work on the principle of purifying air by passing it through filters. Having passed through the filters it is cooled by a water spray. Water vapour is then removed by eliminator plates and the air is then heated to the required temperature. This is necessary, otherwise the air would be too cold.

ICE RINK

The floor of an ice rink is covered with a network of pipes through which cold brine is circulated. Our model shows the refrigeration engine room (top) and the circulatory system. The floor beneath the rink has layers of concrete, waterproofing material, sand and a top layer of concrete containing the pipes.

decay. The use of cold stores means that we can have many varieties of fruit and vegetables throughout the year.

Before fruit is deep frozen ready for transporting, it is often pre-frozen to 0°C (32°F) when picked. This is so that the fruit can then be picked when it is completely ripe.

Meat storage and distribution also make much use of cold. After the animals have been slaughtered, the meat is placed in a chilling chamber at 7°C (45°F) for several hours. The meat can then be sold

straight to the butcher or consumer or kept for a long time in a large refrigerating store. It is essential to keep the meat very cold – sometimes below −10°C (14°F) – since the action of the bacteria is slowed down by the cold. The humidity or the amount of water in the atmosphere of the cold store is carefully controlled. If the air is too dry, the meat dries out.

The processing of dairy products depends on refrigeration at some time or other. Butter needs cold both during manufacture and pre-

servation. Milk needs refrigeration both during pasteurization and its subsequent storing at 5°C (41°F). Cheese does not require cooling during its manufacture but the storing of cheeses for maturing requires strict control of temperature and humidity.

Eggs freeze at −0·6°C (30·9°F) so they are stored at between 1°C (34°F) and −0·5°C (31·1°F). Attention is also given to humidity, for if the atmosphere is too dry, air pockets form within the egg; if too moist, mould forms on the shell.

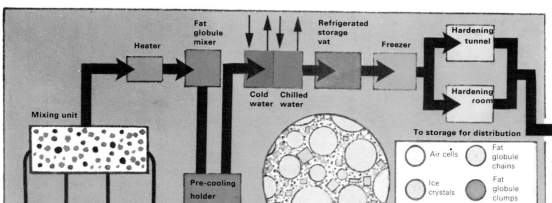

ICE-CREAM

The materials are mixed in a tank and from there go to a heater and then to a mixer which disperses fat globules to a correct proportion. It then goes through a set of cooling processes and then passes through a hardening tunnel and room. It then goes into storage for ultimate distribution. The large circle shows the structure of ice-cream.

Cold and industry

Making things cold or even cool is a complicated science requiring considerable knowledge and skill. Cold is as essential in many industrial processes as heat. Let us take one simple process as an example. Cold water is used in making soap. The hot soap is sprayed onto cylinders containing a stream of very cold water. This cools the soap down rapidly and enables it to form flakes.

Cold is also essential in the manufacture of certain explosives. When nitroglycerine – a very powerful explosive – is made, a freezing mixture of calcium chloride solution at $-15°C$ ($5°F$) allows the reaction of acids and a glycerol-glycol mixture to proceed steadily and safely.

During the processing of petroleum to obtain lubricating oils the waxy impurities have to be removed. This is done by using a very low temperature of $-20°C$ ($-4°F$).

But the most important function of low temperatures in heavy industry is to assist in the separation of gases from various mixtures. Among the gas mixtures separated by cooling and liquefaction are air, coke-oven gas, oil refinery gases and pure hydrogen.

Liquefied air and other gases are now being used in vast quantities. This liquid form is obtained by using high pressures at very low temperatures. Steelworks, for instance, use thousands of tonnes of liquid oxygen every day to remove carbon from iron. Liquid oxygen results from cooling air to about $-190°C$ ($-310°F$). The oxygen in the air liquefies at this temperature but other gases do not.

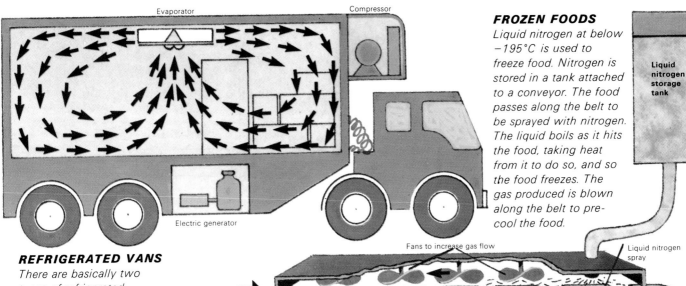

Evaporator · **Compressor**

Electric generator

FROZEN FOODS

Liquid nitrogen at below −195°C is used to freeze food. Nitrogen is stored in a tank attached to a conveyor. The food passes along the belt to be sprayed with nitrogen. The liquid boils as it hits the food, taking heat from it to do so, and so the food freezes. The gas produced is blown along the belt to pre-cool the food.

Liquid nitrogen storage tank

Fans to increase gas flow · **Liquid nitrogen spray** · **Conveyor belt**

REFRIGERATED VANS

There are basically two types of refrigerated trucks - one for fresh meat and vegetables and one for ice-cream and frozen food. Heat is taken up by the liquid in the evaporator.

METHANE ON THE MOVE

Methane gas in the Sahara is cooled to a liquid (−162°C or −260°F) for transportation to Europe. Tankers such as Methane Princess *(below) are used for this. Icy pipes (left) show how cold the gas is.*

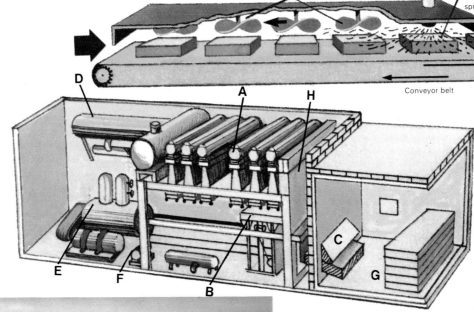

ICE MAKING

In a typical ice making unit the ice is formed in a series of jacketed moulds which are filled with pre-cooled water from an overhead tank. Cold brine circulates in the jacket and into "needles" which cool the centre first. The ice blocks are ejected into a harvester which tips them into a storage room.

A	Jacketed moulds
B	Harvester unit
C	Chute
D	Condenser
E	Compressor
F	Motor
G	Storage room
H	Water tank

Still · **Vapour** · **Liebig condenser** · **Water outlet** · **Water inlet** · **Receiver**

CONDENSER

A Liebig condenser is used to purify a mixed liquid where the contents have widely different boiling points. The liquid is heated in a still to a vapour. It passes into the condenser. The fraction with the lowest boiling point becomes liquid first.

Liquid hydrogen and liquid oxygen are both used in large quantities by space engineers. Hundreds of tonnes of oxygen, liquid paraffin and hydrogen are used to boost the huge Saturn V rockets out of the gravitational field of the earth and into space.

When coal and oil are burned in conventional electric power stations the heat generated is used to heat water to make steam to turn turbogenerators. This steam is then cooled back to water in huge cooling towers. To transport it to the areas where it is needed, the electricity made in this way has its voltage – or power – stepped up to very high levels (around 132,000 volts). The voltage has then to be reduced before the power can be used in the home or in industry. This process is done by transformers, which produce more heat inside the transformers. This heat is subsequently removed by special coolants.

Cold can also be used to transform a gas, such as methane, into a liquid, for ease of transportation in tankers.

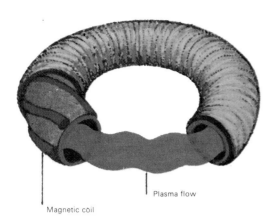

Magnetic coil

Plasma flow

PLASMA VESSEL

During a thermo-nuclear reaction hydrogen plasma at 10,000,000°C is held in a vessel of super-magnetic material at cryogenic temperatures. The magnetism restricts the plasma to the tube's centre, away from the walls, otherwise the vessel would disintegrate.

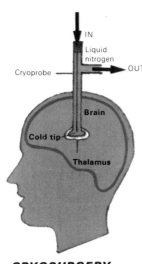

IN

Liquid nitrogen

OUT

Cryoprobe

Brain

Cold tip

Thalamus

CRYOSURGERY

Cold is used for brain surgery and cancer removal. A cryoprobe is inserted and the infected area injected with liquid nitrogen. The damaged cells are killed by deep freezing with no blood loss or pain.

EXPANSION ENGINE

Right: This changes a gas to a liquid. The gas is compressed and then allowed to expand. This cools it. The cold gas then chills the incoming gas more until the temperature is so low the gas becomes a liquid.

MICROSCOPE

Left: This works when a beam of electrons is focused by a magnetic lens onto a screen. It can magnify cells to 100,000 times their size. Cryogenic super-conductivity would increase magnification to 300,000 times.

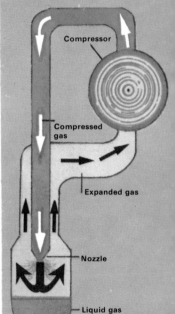

Compressor

Compressed gas

Expanded gas

Nozzle

Liquid gas

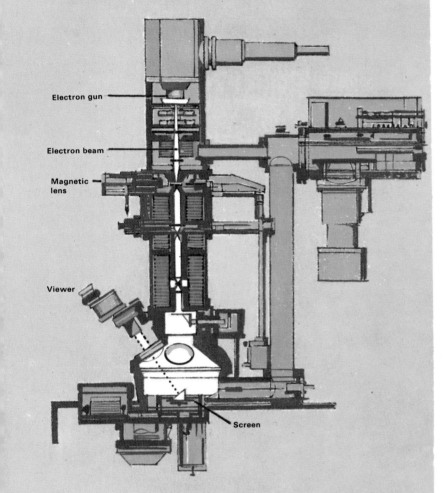

Electron gun

Electron beam

Magnetic lens

Viewer

Screen

Cryogenics~or supercold

The coldest possible temperature to which any substance can be reduced is $-273.15°C$. This coldest point is known as $0°K$, or Absolute Zero, after the great Scottish scientist Lord Kelvin who was the first person to establish this point. At this temperature all matter, except liquid helium, is in a solid state. No one, incidentally, has ever succeeded in cooling anything to Absolute Zero.

In recent years a new science called cryogenics has been developed. This is the study of very low temperatures, particularly of those temperatures where air becomes a liquid. This occurs at around $-200°C$ ($-328°F$), or $73°K$. When we consider that a piece of steel cooled to $-250°C$ ($-418°F$) would shatter like glass we can get some idea of how cold this really is.

In industrial processes the value of extreme cold is considerable. Copper, for example, is a good conductor of electricity. At low temperatures its capacity as a conductor increases. But some substances offer no resistance to electricity at these 'cryogenic' temperatures – mercury, tin and aluminium are examples – and they become superconductors allowing electric motors to run at almost 100 per cent efficiency at a temperature of $4°K$.

A cryogenically cooled ruby crystal, whose atoms were made to vibrate by incoming electromagnetic signals, made it possible for us to receive information from Mars sent back by Mariner IV's fly-past. The information was relayed over 214,000,000 kms (134,000,000 miles) by a microwave radio with a power

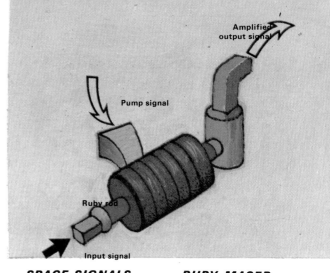

SPACE SIGNALS
A radio telescope at the Onsala Space Observatory in Sweden. This contains a maser amplifier, chilled to near absolute zero by a liquid helium refrigerator. In these conditions the maser can pick up very faint signals from space.

RUBY MASER
This works (above) by using a cryogenically cooled ruby crystal. The crystal's atoms vibrate when radio or other waves pass through it. The excited atoms emit radiation which can be analyzed. The maser is pumped with energy before use.

LASER BEAM
Light can also be produced from a cryogenically cooled ruby crystal. This is a laser (above). Light from a photo-flash tube hits the ruby atoms. This excites their electrons making them emit their own light. When a shutter is released at one end the light shoots out as a powerful beam.

DEWAR VESSEL
This is used for storing very cold liquid gases. It consists of several vessels, usually glass, with a vacuum in between. The inside of the outer vessel has a shiny metal coat to prevent heat absorption. Charcoal placed in the vacuum absorbs any of the residual gas.

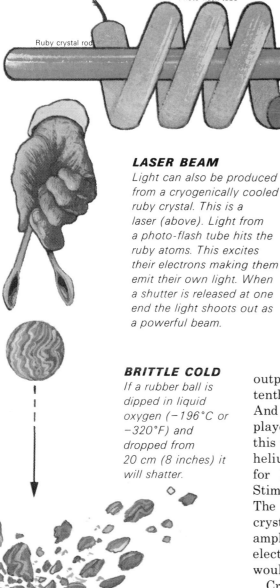

BRITTLE COLD
If a rubber ball is dipped in liquid oxygen (−196°C or −320°F) and dropped from 20 cm (8 inches) it will shatter.

output of only ten watts – about one tenth that of an ordinary light bulb. And this is where the ruby crystal played its part. For the strength of this tiny signal was amplified by a helium cooled maser (maser stands for Microwave Amplification by Stimulated Emission of Radiation). The radiation given out by the crystal receiving the signals was amplified and analyzed without any electrical noise interference, which would have destroyed the signal.

Cryogenics are also used to generate a light ray from a refrigerated ruby crystal. This light is called a laser beam and its highly concentrated light waves can drill holes in any substance in a thousandth of a second. A laser beam the thickness of a pencil can also carry millions of telephone calls.

Cryosurgery, by using special probes, can treat cancer and tumours and even remove tonsils. This can be done without bleeding or infection since the extreme cold stops the blood loss and also sterilizes the surgical probes – a great advance in modern medicine.

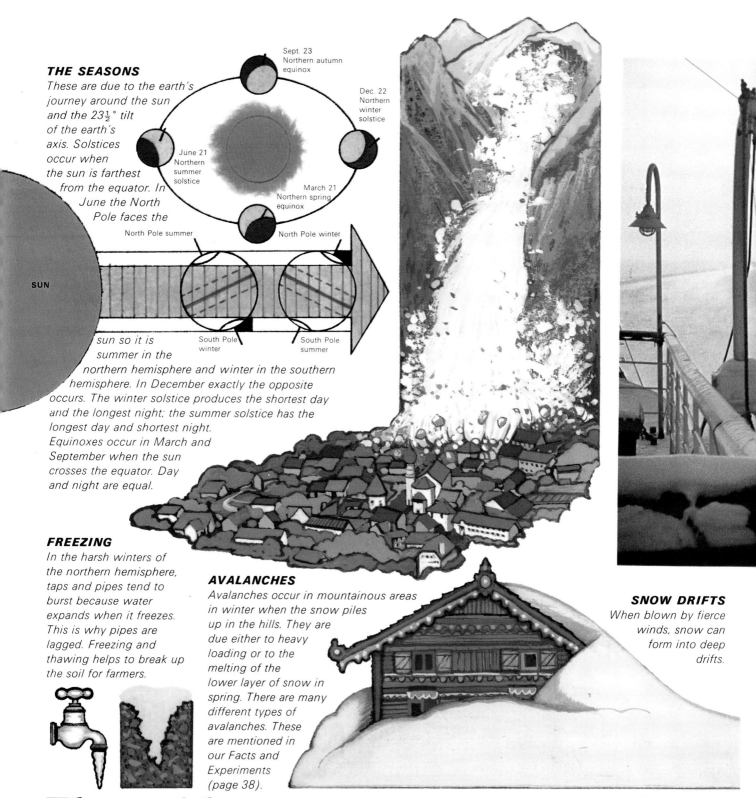

THE SEASONS

These are due to the earth's journey around the sun and the 23½° tilt of the earth's axis. Solstices occur when the sun is farthest from the equator. In June the North Pole faces the sun so it is summer in the northern hemisphere and winter in the southern hemisphere. In December exactly the opposite occurs. The winter solstice produces the shortest day and the longest night; the summer solstice has the longest day and shortest night. Equinoxes occur in March and September when the sun crosses the equator. Day and night are equal.

Sept. 23
Northern autumn equinox

Dec. 22
Northern winter solstice

June 21
Northern summer solstice

March 21
Northern spring equinox

North Pole summer

North Pole winter

SUN

South Pole winter

South Pole summer

FREEZING

In the harsh winters of the northern hemisphere, taps and pipes tend to burst because water expands when it freezes. This is why pipes are lagged. Freezing and thawing helps to break up the soil for farmers.

AVALANCHES

Avalanches occur in mountainous areas in winter when the snow piles up in the hills. They are due either to heavy loading or to the melting of the lower layer of snow in spring. There are many different types of avalanches. These are mentioned in our Facts and Experiments (page 38).

SNOW DRIFTS

When blown by fierce winds, snow can form into deep drifts.

The cold season

It is a curious fact that if you live in the northern hemisphere you are actually about five million kilometres (three million miles) *nearer* to the sun when you are shivering in the depths of winter than you are when you are basking in the sunshine in the middle of summer. In the middle of winter we have less than half the daylight we have in summer, yet the length of the day is just the same – 24 hours. Why do we have winter and why, when it is winter in the northern hemisphere, is it summer in the south?

To understand winter we must know a little about the earth in its relationship to the sun. It takes the earth 365 days, six hours, nine minutes and ten seconds to travel round the sun. The extra hours and minutes are added to a year every four years to make a leap year.

During its journey the earth is tilted towards and away from the sun. In summer in the northern hemisphere, the earth is tilted towards the sun and starts tilting away from it on 21 June, which we call the summer solstice. Three

months before this, on 21 March, and then on 23 September, the lengths of day and night are about the same and there is no tilting of either the North or South Pole towards the sun. On 22 December the winter solstice occurs, when the northern hemisphere is most inclined away from the sun. The effects on daylight duration are most noticeable at the poles. On and around 21 June, the North Pole has 24 hours of light and at the South Pole there is 24 hours darkness. This is reversed on 22 December.

The Baltic has special problems in winter. It is so narrow and shallow that it is rather like a lake, and its water contains little salt. This means it freezes easily. It has also a poor marine life; Baltic herrings are small and the Baltic cod weighs about one fifth of those found off the coast of Norway.

ICE STRUCTURES

In countries which have very severe winters fantastic structures can be made from snow and ice. The Russians once shot a cannon ball of ice from an ice cannon. Here we show an ice building at the 1972 Tokyo Olympics.

AIR POCKETS

Since snow is full of air pockets a man buried in a drift can breathe. Snow is also a good insulator.

PLANTS

A layer of light snow is useful in cold areas since in severe winters it protects plants from soil freeze.

The distances of the earth from the sun means that there is six per cent more heat reaching the earth in December than in June. This means that the winters in the northern hemisphere are more moderate than those in the southern. The effect of this extra energy is less noticeable as you go farther north, because the curve of the earth decreases the heat and light intensities. It is the angle of tilt of the earth's surface to the sun which determines the coming of winter, and its severity depends on where we are living on the earth.

The coldest part of a northern winter is not towards the end of December but in early February, because heat stored in the earth's surface during the summer and autumn is gradually lost in the earlier winter months, tending to lessen the effects of the shorter days. Although there is this six per cent more heat available over the shorter day, a further factor keeping out solar energy is the earth's greater cloud cover in winter, which reflects much of the solar energy.

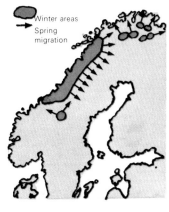

REINDEER
*are one of the few large
animals that migrate.
They live mainly on the
northern tundras, and with
the coming of winter
move south to feed on
lichen, grass and herbs.*

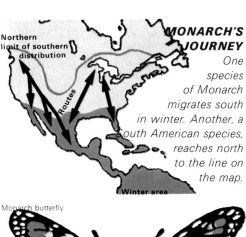

**MONARCH'S
JOURNEY**
*One
species
of Monarch
migrates south
in winter. Another, a
South American species,
reaches north
to the line on
the map.*

Monarch butterfly

**SLEEPY
BEARS**
*Bears are not true
hibernators but in cold
climates some species be-
come fat at the onset of winter.
In severe weather the brown
bear sleeps a lot but wakens up
when it feels hungry or when the
weather relents a little.*

Hibernation and migration

Winter, of course, means that less food is available for the animals and birds. Only a few of the more advanced mammals actually store food and they often forget where they have hidden it! Small animals are unable to store much fat within their bodies to keep them active during the months of short food supply. There are only three alternatives – to move away to a warmer place, go into a deep sleep or die.

When we think of migration, we think first of birds but many mammals migrate over short distances in the late autumn, usually from high in the mountains to lower slopes. The reindeer of Europe is known as the caribou in North America, and it is a migrating animal. The polar and sub-polar regions which support it in the short northern summer are too harsh for it in winter.

The big whales of the Southern Ocean around Antarctica are only able to feed during the southern summer months of November to March or April because their feeding waters freeze over as winter advances. They migrate into the Atlantic, Pacific and Indian oceans.

The Alaskan fur seal breeds mainly on the Pribilof Islands and on the Commander Islands. After the breeding season, the fur seals migrate in three main directions – to the islands of Japan, the Californian coast and to the Aleutian Islands. They return to their breeding stations in May.

Hundreds of species of butterflies and moths also migrate. The best known American migrant butterfly is the monarch which is found

SO SNUG

Dormice sleep for as long as six months at a time in nests they make for themselves. They curl themselves up so tightly that they can be rolled about!

INSECTS

In winter, beetles, flies and many other insects and larvae sleep in the bark of trees and in the soil. (Right) larva of a cockchafer.

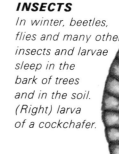

ARCTIC TERNS

nest in the high latitudes of the northern hemisphere in summer but fly to areas in the South Pacific and Atlantic oceans for winter, sometimes as far south as Antarctica.

Migration routes

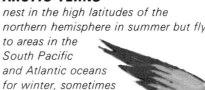

STORING FOOD

Squirrels may lie up for a day or two in winter when the weather is bad, but they do not hibernate. They hide their surplus food among the leaf litter.

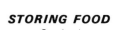

SNAKES,

like most cold-blooded animals, hibernate in winter. They sleep in old burrows, below the frostline.

Burrow

throughout the United States and southern Canada, and even as far north as Hudson Bay. Its migrations are spectacular, several millions flying off together. They travel south to Florida and Texas in September and go into hibernation there until the following March, arriving back in the north at the beginning of June, a return journey of well over 3200 km (2100 miles).

The world record for the largest migrations is held by the little Arctic tern which breeds in the Arctic and then travels as far as Australia and Antarctica. These annual round trips total more than 29,000 km (18,000 miles).

Some mammals that cannot migrate must hibernate to survive the winter. Many small animals such as bats, dormice and hedgehogs spend most of the winter in a deep sleep. During this time their body temperature falls to 18°C (64°F) or it may be as low as 2°C (36°F). The sleep is usually stimulated by cold and the drop in body temperature slows the body mechanisms to a minimum to conserve energy.

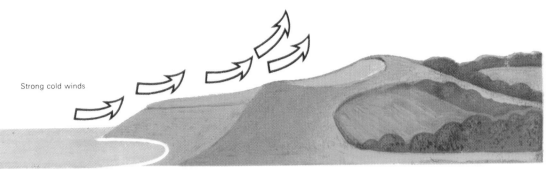

Strong cold winds

COASTLINE TREES

Few trees grow round the coastline, except where surrounding cliffs and hills provide shelter. This is due to strong, cold winds blowing off the seas. Trees which do grow on the coast often show marked stunting of growth.

TREELINE

Trees do not grow beyond a certain altitude. This limit of growth is called the treeline and it varies with temperature and climate. As our chart shows, the treeline round the equator is higher than that of temperate New Zealand. In colder Britain the treeline is lower.

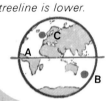

A. Equator, 2000 metres (6600 ft) warm

B. New Zealand, 1200 metres (4000 ft) cooler

C. Britain, 600 metres (2000 ft) cold

NORTH ATLANTIC DRIFT
WARM WESTERLIES

SOUTH GEORGIA

COLD WINDS

FALKLAND CURRENT

COLD WINDS

TREELESS ISLAND

There are no trees on South Georgia, an island off the coast of South America, because the incoming winds are cooled by the very cold Falkland current. The coast of Britain, on the other hand, is warmed by the westerlies which blow over the warm North Atlantic drift. This promotes tree growth.

THE WIND LINE

Right: We have all seen trees on exposed sites leaning away from the prevailing wind. This is partly due to the consistent pressure of the wind, but it is also the tree's attempt to evade the cold which stunts its growth on that side. This wind-blown pine is growing on a Scottish moor.

FOOD STORES

Many plants, which grow in cold weather or cool shady areas, store food in special roots such as bulbs, corms, tubers and rhizomes. We show, from left to right, a crocus corm, iris rhizome and a daffodil bulb.

Cold and plants

Cold has very marked and visible effects on plants and plant distribution. To take some simple examples, the south side of a hill is generally warmer and less windswept than the northern side. Oak trees in a valley will produce acorns every year, but those trees rooted higher up the slopes are affected by late spring frosts which kill the flower buds. The actual growth of the tree is also stunted.

Many botanists believe that most, if not all, flowering plant species evolved in tropical areas and adaptation to the cooler, temperate, and cold polar climates came later. The ability to lose leaves is an adaptation. Plants from the tropics cannot survive in temperate zones unless they are very carefully protected from the cold winds and frost, or grown indoors in a glass house. Similarly, polar and alpine plants suffer if kept in too warm a climate.

Winds blowing off the seas have a marked effect on the growth of trees. In fact, they are very often absent on coastlines, except where shelter is provided by the surrounding cliffs and hills. Trees growing within a few kilometres of the sea are often stunted and bent. There is also a limit, known as the tree line, to the altitude at which trees can grow. This is not at the same height all over the world, or on any particular hillside or mountain. At or near the equator trees can grow at a height of about 2000 metres (6600 ft). In New Zealand the tree line occurs at about 1200 metres (4000 ft), while in Britain it is at 600 metres (2000 ft), except in the Scottish Highlands. South Georgia

LEAF FALL

Deciduous trees also hibernate in winter. Roots stop taking up water, a layer of cork grows between leaf and stem and the leaves fall to reduce evaporation. A thick bark layer may grow on the cold side of the tree.

Sap

Cork

Cold side

FROST WITHER

Spring frosts can be a menace to burgeoning leaves and buds. This twig shows the withered effect of frostbite on a leaf and typical discoloration. Whole trees can wilt after severe frost. Potatoes can be killed in very cold weather unless they are protected from the frosts.

occupies a similar position of latitude south of the equator as Britain does to the north and yet there are no trees there. The reason for this is because the British coast and incoming westerly winds are warmed by the warm sea current called the North Atlantic Drift, while South Georgia lies right in the path of the very cold Falklands current from the Antarctic.

Below 3 – 5°C (37 – 41°F) most plants cannot make food from sunlight. Alpine plants can manage between 5°C (41°F) and 10°C (50°F), while temperate plants growing in woodlands need from about 15°C (59°F) to about 18°C (64°F).

Deciduous trees with their broad leaves cast deep shadows, making the air below cool and moist. Many plants have adapted to these conditions and develop and flower early in the year. This means that much of the growing goes on in cold weather, with perhaps night frosts. To help them, many of these plants build up food stores in special organs such as bulbs, corms, rhizomes and tubers.

TURN COAT!

For camouflage and to reduce heat loss in winter, the coats of animals in Arctic areas often turn white in winter. We show the stoat's winter coat and its brown summer coat.

FIRM FOOTING

The feet of reindeer living on the icy tundra are much wider than their grass-land relatives, the fallow deer. Broad feet help the animal to grip the frozen earth and snow.

Fallow deer

Reindeer

Arctic fox

Reindeer Caribou

Common seal

Musk ox

Not to scale

SNOWSHOE

The snowshoe rabbit - so called because of its thick, hairy foot pads — lives mainly in the north of America. Its broad feet provide a firm grip on the soft snow, as do snowshoes for man. The coat of the snowshoe rabbit turns white during winter.

FOX MASKS

To cut down heat loss from the body many polar animals have small ears and muzzles. Compare the various foxes below.

POLAR ANIMALS

This map of the tundra and Arctic areas of the northern hemisphere indicates the broad distribution pattern of the common species of animals living in these areas. You can see where they are to be found by checking the coloured dots on our map and referring to the key below. Of course, many other animals are to be found in these areas but these are the main varieties. There are no penguins at the North Pole.

Desert fox

Common fox

Arctic fox

Cold and animals

Animals have an inbuilt clock which tells them when winter is coming. The shortening of the length of the day and the gradual dropping in temperature often triggers off the growth of longer hair to protect them against the cold. The fat stored beneath their skin increases and this acts as a barrier against the cold from without and helps their bodies to retain heat. It also acts as an extra food reserve when times get really hard.

Birds often have to change their diet in winter. Kestrels will take butterflies, small mammals and even worms in summer, but when these are not available it will concentrate on catching small birds. Blackbirds and thrushes will eat small invertebrates such as worms and snails in a mixed summer diet. During the colder months they feed almost solely on the remaining seeds and fruits they can find.

The Arctic foxes have a greyish-yellow summer coat. As winter comes along their fur turns white. Their muzzles and ears are shorter than in other foxes. This helps to cut down body heat loss. They have long coats which they need and, to help them walk on the snow and ice, there are long hairs on the soles of their feet.

On the other hand, the polar bear is white throughout the year, moving south with the pack ice in the summer and returning northwards when it breaks up. They, too, have small ears, thick fur and hairs under the feet. The feet are very large to help spread their tremendous weight, up to 500 kg (half a ton), as they walk over ice and snow. They

POLAR BEARS

Polar bears have thick fur and a deep layer of fat to protect them from the intense cold of the polar regions. Like most polar animals they have big paws which provide extra grip on the ice. They are poor swimmers and travel round the Arctic mainly on ice floes.

Lemming   Adelie penguin   Albatross   Emperor Penguin   Killer whale   Elephant seal   Polar bear

ANTARCTICA

This map shows the animals and birds most common in the Antarctic. See the colour key again.

FOOD FOR SLEEP

This fat little dormouse has, like most hibernating animals, stored fat for the long winter sleep.

can swim but travel mostly by hitching lifts on ice floes.

Alpine and Scottish hares and snowshoe rabbits also turn white in winter although this has been shown to be in response to the shortening length of the day and not to the cold. Hares lie up in the daytime in small hollows or in tussocks of grass and in the winter in a hollow pressed out in the snow, sheltered from the wind. The snowshoe rabbit, which is really a hare, has a hairy mat on each foot to help it grip the snow.

Ptarmigans make use of white plumage both for camouflage and for a reduction in body heat loss. They are found all round the Arctic and in the Pyrenees, Alps, and on top of mountains, which suggests that they may be something of a relic species from the Ice Ages that have retreated northwards and upwards since the retreat of the glaciers. They are well adapted to survive in the cold. They are able to burrow into snow for shelter and also have heavily feathered toes which act as efficient snowshoes.

Facts and experiments

THE WORLD UNDER WATER

Since one tenth of the world is covered by ice the effect on mankind if all the ice melted would be dramatic. Most of this ice stretches across the 1,800,000 sq. kms (700,000 sq. miles) of Greenland and the 13,000,000 sq. kms (5,000,000 sq. miles) of Antarctica. If all this ice were to melt the level of the seas would rise by about 76 metres (250 feet), swamping all the world's harbours and many of its principal cities. The Panama Canal would become a strait and the Suez Canal would vanish. The Bering Strait between Alaska and the USSR would widen, allowing more warm water to sweep into the Arctic and channelling cold water down the west coast of America. Most of England would vanish apart from the Cotswolds, Mendips, Chilterns and Downs. Only the tips of the New York skyscrapers would peep above the waves but Australia and Africa would be relatively unharmed. Rainfall would be re-distributed and Continental areas could experience drought. Such a melting could shift the poles and start another Ice Age due to more water vapour – and hence more snow.

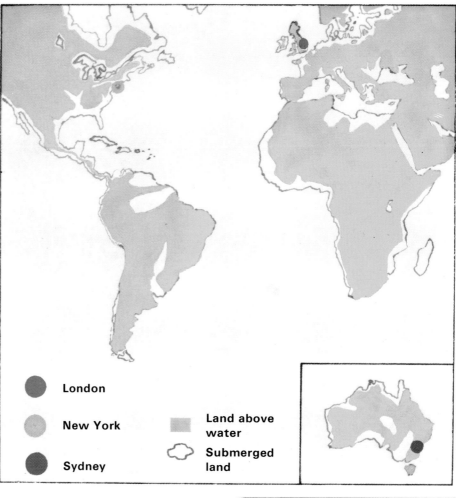

- London
- New York
- Sydney
- Land above water
- Submerged land

But, apart from the submerging of vast areas of land, the effect would be a return to the conditions experienced just before the great Ice Ages. Air temperatures in both high and low latitudes would be very similar. The temperature of the Arctic would rise by 5–10°C in summer and by 2·5°–5°C in winter. The Antarctic summer would be warmer than the Arctic but its winters would be more severe. There could even be a return to sub-tropical vegetation in the lower latitudes and there would be mass migrations of birds and animals towards the north. The warming of the sea would have a pronounced effect on the pattern of sea life. For example, during the warmer phase of the early part of this century the cod, herring and haddock suddenly appeared off the Greenland coast. As the climate became cooler in the 1960s, the catch dropped dramatically. In some land areas there would be a big increase in the agricultural growing season.

IRISH SNAKES

The snakes in Ireland were not banished by St Patrick, as the legend tells us, but by the Ice Age which covered Ireland in a sheet of ice.

New York

If the Poles melted, the Statue of Liberty (90 m) would be chest deep.

Sydney

The Opera House (62 m) would be swamped by the 76 m rise.

London

Water would touch the dome of St Paul's Cathedral (114 m).

MOVING POLES

It is not impossible for the position of the poles to change – in fact, it has happened before. This alone could cause a melting of the ice caps. If the North Pole were situated in the area of the Northern Pacific and the South Pole were directly opposite in the South Atlantic, there could be no ice. The ocean currents would mix warm equatorial water with that of the polar regions. All this is perfectly possible. Even the continents have changed their positions in the past.

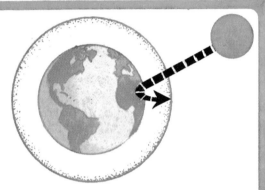

HEAT BLANKET

Other scientists believe the ice could melt for another reason. The amount of carbon dioxide in the air is rising and the rapid increase in the burning of fossilized fuels such as coal, oil and gas will, they believe, create a blanket of carbon dioxide round the earth. This would reduce the amount of heat radiating back into space.

SUN SPOTS

One popular theory is that the melting and freezing of the world's ice might be due to changes in the amount of radiation reaching the earth from the sun. It is believed that sun spots, which fluctuate in size and number, have been the cause of many recent changes in the earth's climate and temperature and could have caused the great ice ages of the past.

'JUNGLES' AT THE POLES

Thousands of years ago, before the Pleistocene ice sheet spread across one fifth of the earth, sub-tropical vegetation grew as far north and as far south as the polar regions. Since the great ice cap retreated 10,000 years ago there have been many changes in our climate. Between 4000 and 2000 years BC temperatures were several degrees warmer and the sea level two metres (six feet) higher. Around AD 1000 the Arctic ice sheet shrank and made it possible for the Vikings to voyage to Greenland and America. Even in our times temperatures have fluctuated. We show an artist's impression of England's Thames valley in a glacial and interglacial phase.

FROZEN THAMES

There have been many cold phases during the last few centuries. In Tudor and Napoleonic times the winters were much colder. The Thames often froze solidly and oxen were roasted on the ice. The last time the Thames froze to this extent was in fact in Victorian times – in 1855. Severe winters are often referred to in the plays of Shakespeare. Today there are signs of another cool phase.

THE RIVER THAMES, FROZEN.—SKETCHED NEAR SHAD THAMES.

Facts and experiments

ICE TEST

You can easily check that water expands when it freezes. If you have a soft polythene – NOT glass – bottle with a screw top, fill it to the top with water and place it in the freezer of your refrigerator for about six hours or in a freezing mixture of ice and salt for an hour. Then look at the result. The bottle will have swollen. A glass bottle would shatter which is why you must only do this experiment with a plastic bottle. If you let the frozen plastic bottle stand in a warm room for half an hour or so and look at it every five minutes you can see it slowly regain its original shape.

ICE AND PRESSURE

Did you know that ice melts more rapidly under pressure? This is one reason why skaters seem to glide across the ice. The ice melts at the point of contact of the skates. We can prove the effect of pressure on ice by a very simple experiment. If you can find a block of ice (even a large ice-cube from the fridge will do) and suspend a wire across it with weights at either end, the wire will melt its way through.

ICE CREAM

Ice "cream" was known in the days of the Roman Empire. Some of it was made from the winter snow which gathers around the lava cones of the active volcano, Mount Etna, in Italy. Huge blocks of ice were carved out of the caves and carried down the mountainside by mules. Fruit juice and sugar were then mixed with the ice. Marco Polo, the great Venetian explorer (1254–1324) who travelled from Venice to China and back, is said to have brought back a recipe for milk ices.

AVALANCHES

Avalanches occur when masses of snow suddenly break loose from the mountainside and plunge down the slopes. They are most common in winter and spring and on slopes with a gradient of 22 degrees or more. Sometimes the snow builds up to such a dangerous level that it takes only a human voice or slight breeze to trigger off an avalanche. The avalanche begins as a powdery cloud but becomes thick and heavy near the base of the slope as the rocks, soil and boulders are caught up in its path. The force of this 'moving mountain' can destroy an entire village although a lot of the damage may be caused by an unexplained wind, called an avalanche blast. The effects of this blast can be just as devastating as the actual avalanche and can often cause more damage. One avalanche blast threw an iron bridge 50 metres (164 ft) into the air. In 1689 the small town of Graas, in the Swiss Alps, was completely smothered by an avalanche.

COLD AS A PRESERVATIVE

Cold in any shape or form is a splendid preservative. We have already pointed out that the great hairy mammoths of the Ice Age were perfectly preserved in deep, icy crevasses. And in Antarctica, where the cold is so intense and precipitation almost entirely in the form of snow, objects also decay very slowly. For example, huts built for expeditions of more than 70 years ago are still in a perfect state. And in one area there is a form of penguin burial ground where a shallow deposit of whole, dried penguins can be found. Some of these remains are thought to be more than 1000 years old.

SEA ICE

Sea water is much harder to freeze than fresh water. This is because salt lowers the freezing point of water. A fresh-water lake has only to cool to 4°C (39°F) throughout before the surface begins to ice over but the bulk of the sea water mass has to cool well below zero before the surface layers freeze. Waves and tidal motion also prevent the calm conditions necessary for the surface of the ice to congeal into a relatively thick ice sheet. Sea ice usually forms in river estuaries where the salt level is low or in protected bays where the waves are slight. It occurs in the Northern Baltic where the tidal motion is weak. When sea water does freeze, ice crystals begin to form round nuclei in the water. As the crystals grow and interlock they take up water around the nuclei and squeeze out much of the salt. The summer thaw helps to wash most of the surface salt away, so when polar ice is more than a year old it is almost fresh when melted. When the ice crystals first start they form 'slush'. If they continue to grow, an 'ice rind' or thin elastic crust develops. To prove fresh water freezes faster than salt water, fill two plastic cups with tap water. Place a teaspoon of salt in one (indicated by yellow label) and leave them in the freezer for two hours. The container with the fresh water will have more ice after that time than that with the brine.

ICE CRYSTAL

This is a drawing of what ice looks like under the microscope. The principle of an ice crystal is simple. Each crystal consists of water molecules held together by hydrogen bonds. These bonds are formed by the attraction which exists between the hydrogen atoms of each molecule and the oxygen atoms of other molecules. The actual shape of individual ice crystals depends on how cold the ice is.

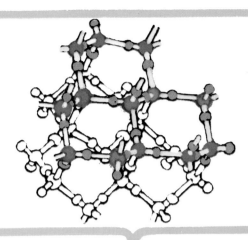

PERMAFROST

This is the name given to land that remains frozen for more than two years. In the northern hemisphere the area of continuously frozen land occupies almost 7,680,000 sq. kms (three million square miles) and in the southern hemisphere the whole of Antarctica is permanently frozen. The thickest permafrost occurs in the Antarctic and Greenland ice caps where the ground can be frozen to depths of 1000 metres (3300 ft). Some areas of permafrost have a surface thaw during the summer but the deeper layers remain frozen. Permafrost areas present great problems in mining, the creation of air-strips, roads and general building. The permafrost in Northern Siberia reaches down to 600 metres (2000 ft). In Canada and Northern Alaska it reaches 450 metres (1500 ft). Our map shows northern permafrost areas.

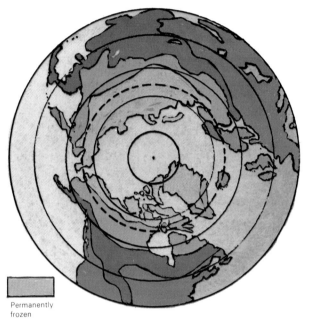

Permanently frozen

Occasionally frozen

Semi-permanent

Active layer

Permafrost

CHANNEL GLACIER

The English channel was once a glacier. About 150,000 years ago the Channel glacier was at the south-western edge of Europe's ice sheet. The glacier flowed from the west of Ireland. A great heap of stone and

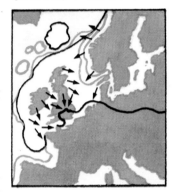

sand at Goodwood, in Sussex, (which is 38 metres or 130 ft above sea level) is thought to be the debris pushed out by the vast Channel glacier during a particularly cold period.

DRY ICE

At normal air temperatures and at atmospheric pressure level, carbon dioxide cannot exist as a liquid, only a gas. Therefore solid carbon dioxide or 'dry ice' turns directly into a vapour. At $-80°C$ ($-112°F$) it is much colder than ice and is used for short term storage such as keeping food cold for aeroplane passengers — thus avoiding the need for powered refrigerators on aircraft. It is also coming into increasing use for the transport of perishable goods by road or rail.

FROST BOIL

Wherever permafrost is formed there is a risk of a curious condition known as 'frost boil'. This occurs when the sub-surface moisture turns into ice and expands. A frost boil can have dramatic results — one of the most commonly seen is the 'drunken forest'; when ice expands it forces its way to the surface and splits the earth. Great pressure results and any trees on the surface are pushed aside to make way for the ice which breaks through the soil. This ice can spread over wide areas and can last a long time.

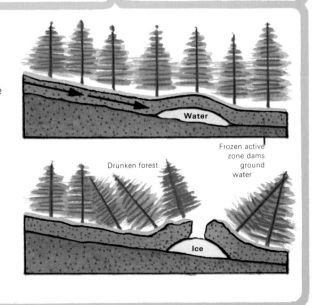

Water

Frozen active zone dams ground water

Drunken forest

Ice

Facts and experiments

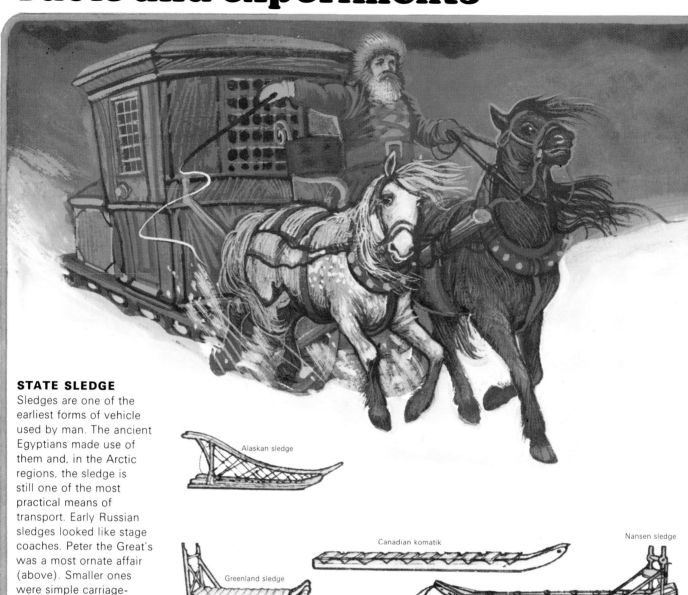

Alaskan sledge

Greenland sledge

Canadian komatik

Nansen sledge

STATE SLEDGE

Sledges are one of the earliest forms of vehicle used by man. The ancient Egyptians made use of them and, in the Arctic regions, the sledge is still one of the most practical means of transport. Early Russian sledges looked like stage coaches. Peter the Great's was a most ornate affair (above). Smaller ones were simple carriage-like affairs.

MAKE YOUR OWN SLEDGE

To make your own sledge you will need the following simple items: Two pieces of prepared softwood, 95 cm (37 inches) long, 15 cm (6 inches) wide and 18 mm (0·7 inch) deep. Four pieces of prepared softwood, 40 cm (15·5 inches) long, 15 cm (6 inches) wide and 18 mm (0·7 inch) deep. Finally, one more piece of prepared softwood should be 75 cm (29·5 inches) long, 15 cm (6 inches) wide and 18 mm (0·7 inch) deep. You will also need 5 cm (2 inch) number eight screws, water-proof glue and varnish and a 1·8 metre (6 feet) length of rope. The sledge is very simple to make – if you follow very carefully the instructions we give below. Look carefully, too, at our picture of the finished model.

1·8 cms
95 cms
15 cms

1·8 cms
40 cms
15 cms

1·8 cms
75 cms
15 cms

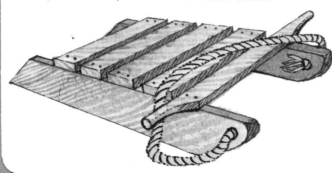

METHOD

Shape the 95 cm lengths, round corners for the front at one end. Shape the 75 cm strip and keep cut-out pieces for strengthening brackets beneath foot rest. Space planks across sides. Glue and screw. Drill holes for rope. Thread and knot. Then varnish completely.

POLAR TRANSPORT

Modern polar vehicles include giant caterpillar tractors, snowmobiles (below), snowcats (below right), a few wheeled vehicles – good in performance on certain surfaces – aerosleds (right) and aeroplanes. Very low temperatures make the operation of mechanical vehicles difficult. Cooling mixtures tend to freeze

SLEDGES

There are many types of sledge (left). Some, such as the Alaskan basket sledge, are simple constructions of thongs and poles. The Nansen sledge, used by Nansen on his polar journeys, is widely used in Arctic regions. Sledges are pulled by reindeer, dogs and horses, depending on where they are used. In the really cold areas dogs have proved unbeatable. Reindeer are used in northern Scandinavia and in Lapland. Horses were used at one time in Russia. Dogs can pull 45 kg (100 lb) for many days on end. Horses can manage 680 kg (1500 lb), ponies about 320 kg (705 lb) and reindeer about 136 kg (300 lb). Amundsen proved the superiority of dogs on his dash to the South Pole. Scott and his men pulled their own sledges and arrived, exhausted, at the Pole — a month later than Amundsen.

ANTI-FREEZE

Anti-freeze mixtures, such as ethylene glycol, are usually added to the water in car radiators during winter. These organic chemicals lower the freezing point of water by several degrees and stop it from freezing in the radiator. It is possible for a car radiator to freeze even when the car is being driven and the water in the engine is hot. A thermostat stops the hot water from circulating through the radiator until the engine reaches a certain temperature. Radiator water can freeze before the thermostat valve opens.

Water flows through the pump and water jacket when the thermostat is closed.

When the thermostat is open the water can pass into the radiator to be cooled.

THE SALT TEST

Place two or three ice cubes in a container. Sprinkle with pinches of salt or put three to five drops of anti-freeze onto them. You will see some of the ice melt very rapidly. This is because the salt in the water gives out some heat. The cube soon dissolves.

RAILWAY HAZARDS

The freezing and icing up of points is a common railway hazard in winter. Electric, gas and propane point heaters, some of which are ignited on site and others by remote control or by thermostats, are used to keep points ice-free. Some points are protected to a degree by a special anti-freeze mixture added to the point lubricant. Other cold weather problems for the railways include heavy snowfalls and snow drifts. Snow ploughs are fixed to the front of locomotives in very cold regions, such as the north of Canada and parts of America, to push the snow aside. Our picture shows a powerful snow plough of this type thrusting through a deep fall of snow.

ICE TOUCH-DOWN

It is a curious fact that heavy, wheeled aircraft can make comfortable landings on firm ice surfaces. The impact of the aircraft's wheels on smooth, glassy ice at well below zero is roughly the same as that made by landing on a concrete airstrip. Ski planes have also proved extremely useful on sludge ice and firm snow in the Arctic areas.

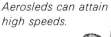
Aerosleds can attain high speeds.

inside the radiator, so air-cooled engines are better. Oil clogs and metal parts can be difficult to handle in very cold conditions. They become brittle and break. Electric batteries produce very little power at sub-zero temperatures and rubber tyres tend to split. Petrol engines involve starting difficulties, battery weakness and fuel evaporation. Diesel oil

engines have a poor power/weight ratio but do not depend on electric batteries. The gas turbine engine is popular today since this is also independent of electric batteries. Its efficiency actually increases in very cold weather.

The snowcat excels in soft snow.

ROCK SALT

Crushed rock salt is often scattered across roads during winter because salt, like ethylene glycol, lowers the freezing point of snow and ice. This increases the rate of melting and prevents the roads from icing up. However, salt rusts the metal body of a car.

Facts and experiments

FOG AND MIST

We all know visibility is often dangerously obscured by mists and fogs but do you know the difference between the two? If we can see to a distance of two kilometres (1·25 miles) we have a mist but if visibility is below one kilometre (1100 yards) we have a fog. Both are due to the condensation of water vapour into droplets that are so small they are actually suspended in the air. Smogs occur when water droplets condense round smoke particles. There are three types of fog and mist. Ground fogs and mists are caused by the direct cooling of the air above a surface temperature below dew point (see DEW AND FROST). They also form over lakes and rivers where the air is saturated with water. Sea mists occur when warm air blows over relatively cold water. These are most common in the spring and summer. When low, moisture-laden clouds are forced to rise over a hill the water condenses to form hill fog and mist. River mists rise to 150 metres (500 ft) and sea mists to about three metres to 30 metres (10 to 100 feet).

DEW AND FROST

Dew is the formation of minute droplets of water on cold surfaces. It occurs on calm, clear nights, when the temperature of the air falls to a level known as 'dew point'. As the temperature drops, the amount of water vapour in the air remains constant but the amount of water the air can hold becomes progressively less with lower temperatures. If the temperature drops to such an extent, water vapour in the air condenses into fine droplets and (below freezing point) to ice and hoar frost.

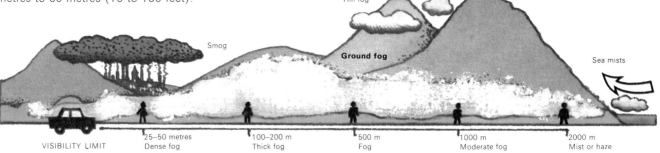

Hill fog

Smog

Ground fog

Sea mists

| VISIBILITY LIMIT | 25–50 metres Dense fog | 100–200 m Thick fog | 500 m Fog | 1000 m Moderate fog | 2000 m Mist or haze |

DAMPNESS

There are many days in Britain when the temperature feels far colder than that shown on the thermometer. This is because Britain experiences a good deal of wet cold. The air becomes cold and humid and this happens mostly when the temperature is near to freezing point. This damp air penetrates our clothing and reduces its insulating powers so that we feel the cold more. This cannot happen below −5°C (23°F) because air saturated with water vapour at this temperature contains hardly any water. Any excess would be in the form of snow and this does not penetrate clothing. In areas such as Canada and Central Europe a drier cold is encountered because winter temperatures usually fall below −5°C.

CLIMBING RULE

One golden rule to be followed when walking on mountains, apart from obvious safety measures, is NEVER wear shorts or jeans. These give very inadequate protection against the wind and rain and they allow dangerous amounts of heat to be lost through the legs. Do not walk too quickly. Too much haste means overheating followed by perspiration and condensation. This chills the skin and muscles. Always be sure to wear strong and waterproof footwear. Without warm feet in a healthy condition, your life could be in jeopardy.

The experienced mountain climber has a woollen hat, scarf, sweater, a windproof jacket, warm gloves, loose woollen pants, thick socks and strong boots.

Correct

ESKIMOS

Eskimos have a rich, fatty, diet high in body heating calories so that they can maintain a high rate of heat production. Their igloos become very hot inside and this helps them to recover from the effects of exposure to the intense cold outside. The Eskimo strips off all his clothes and this allows the heat to soak into the layers of fat that have been protecting him.

CONDENSATION

Pour some hot water into a bowl to a depth of three to four centimetres (1·5 inches). Cover the bowl with some polythene and place in the fridge for ten to fifteen minutes. On removal, notice the number of large water droplets that have condensed from the hot water vapour in the air below the polythene. This is similar to the formation of dew. On cold nights this may freeze and will then form frost.

PEASOUPERS

During the second half of the 19th century and the first half of the 20th century, peasoupers, or heavy smogs, were a feature of the late Industrial Revolution in major British cities. They were caused by water droplets forming round smoke particles. The smogs were so thick they blotted out the noonday sun, and bright lights were invisible at a distance of several metres. Pedestrians used walls to feel their way along the footpaths and often became lost within a few metres from home. The smogs were also harmful to health and were responsible for many deaths from bronchial disease. It was only in 1957, when the Clean Air laws came into force, that London and other large industrial cities became smog-free.

Incorrect

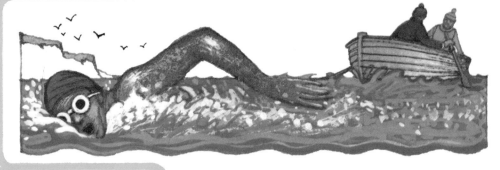

CLO UNIT

There is a unit for measuring clothing insulation. It is called the CLO. One CLO would be registered if a person were to sit comfortably in a room at 21°C (70°F) for a longish period without any rise or fall in body temperature.

LONG DISTANCE SWIMMERS

Long distance swimming is considered to be one of the greatest tests of athletic endurance in the world. This is because water conducts heat away from the body, which rapidly reduces the swimmer's energy and ability. Most long distance swimmers smother themselves with thick grease to reduce heat loss and spend weeks accustoming their bodies to long spells in cold water. A fit, young person can survive in waters of 15°C (59°F) for three to six hours but a drop to 14·5°C (58°F) soon taxes the leg and arm muscles. The heart and other inner organs begin to fail in temperatures of 12·5°C (54·5°F) for, no matter how hard the muscles work, the heat produced is not enough to maintain normal heart activity.

Facts and experiments

ALPINE PLANTS
These plants have many ingenious ways of adapting to the bitter cold and icy winds of the mountain areas. They are usually very small with short stems that enable them to lie almost flat on the ground, out of the wind. Furry, or wax-coated, leaves help to conserve valuable moisture which would be rapidly lost in the dry alpine winds. Some plants, like the Alpine Soldanella (above), thrust their way through the snow.

INSECT ANTI-FREEZE
The body fluids of some insects, such as the pupa of the Cecropia moth (below), contain glycerol, a syrupy liquid that lowers the freezing point of the body fluids. These insects can survive in sub-zero temperatures without their body fluids freezing solid.

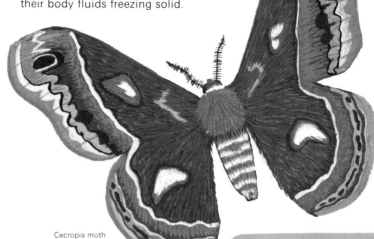

Cecropia moth

WARM FLIPPERS
The flippers of the seal never become cold. The arteries and veins at the junction of the flippers and the body lie so close together that the warm blood, flowing from the internal organs through the arteries, heats up the cool blood coming from the flippers. The seal's body temperature, therefore, remains stable.

DARK INSECTS
Insects in the polar areas are nearly all black in colour, for this helps them absorb heat from the sun. This can be seen when dead insects fall on the snow. The heat absorbed melts a little snow near the body.

OCEAN COLOURS
The oceans of Antarctica are so rich in microscopic plant life, or phytoplankton, that the water becomes a vivid green in some areas. Then again, in other areas, where the sea teems with the tiny marine life or krill (below) which feed off the phytoplankton, the water appears a deep red. Cold water rising from the bottom of the ocean carries mineral salts and other material that the phytoplankton need for growth and food production to the surface. The small, shrimp-like krill congregate in these areas. Sometimes shoals of these little crustacea can be as deep as five to 40 metres (16–130 ft).

WHALE BLUBBER
About 30 tonnes of a 70 tonne whale consist of blubber. The Greenland whale has a coat of fat more than 50 cm (20 inches) thick.

WHITE BLOOD
The fish of the Chaenichthyidae species, which live in the polar seas, have white blood. The blood has no red corpuscles or haemaglobin. As a result their oxygen intake is much less than that of fish with red blood. This makes them suited to life under the ice caps, where the oxygen content is low.

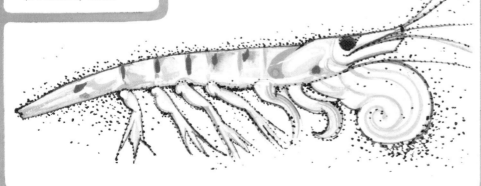

Index

ACKNOWLEDGEMENTS

Antarctic Division photograph by C. Scott
(Dept. of Science, Australia), Ardea
Photographics, Barnaby's Picture Library,
British Antarctic Survey, British Insulated
Callenders Cables Ltd., Canadian Tourist Board,
Bruce Coleman (Jane Burton), Colorsport,
Colour Library International, Crown Copyright
(by kind permission of the Controller,
Her Majesty's Stationery Office), Dr I. Everson,
Findlay Irvine Ltd., Institute of Geological
Sciences, Mansell Collection, Methane
Services Ltd., NERC (reproduced by kind
permission of the Director, Institute of Geological
Sciences), Picturepoint, Radio Times Hulton
Picture Library, S.F. Air Ltd., Spectrum Colour
Library, Swiss National Tourist Office.

Editorial research and assistance: Jane Covernton
Artist: Michael Whittlesea

45

THE PLANETS AND THEIR TEMPERATURES

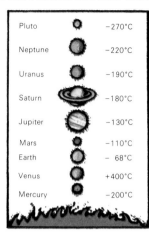

Pluto		−270°C
Neptune		−220°C
Uranus		−190°C
Saturn		−180°C
Jupiter		−130°C
Mars		−110°C
Earth		− 68°C
Venus		+400°C
Mercury		−200°C

With the exception of Venus, all the planets experience temperatures well below zero. On the left we show the estimated minimum temperatures of each planet. The figure for earth was recorded in Northern Siberia. The temperature of Pluto falls to almost Absolute Zero.

Mercury −38·9°C

−117°C Ethyl alcohol (whisky)

Petrol −56·8°C

Milk −

Acetic acid (vinegar) −16·6°C

Water 0°C

Butane −138°C

Eggs −0·6°C

Margarine +30

FREEZING POINTS
Common substances and their freezing points.

GREAT NAMES IN THE STORY OF COLD
SIR JAMES DEWAR (1842–1923)
One of the first scientists to study the properties of matter at temperatures near to Absolute Zero. He was the first man to liquefy oxygen in public. Dewar liquefied gases by reducing their temperature until they condensed. In 1899 he was the first to liquefy hydrogen at −240°C (−400°F). He later succeeded in freezing hydrogen solid. He invented the Dewar vessel, basis of the vacuum flask.

HEIKE KAMERLINGH ONNES (1853–1926)
Dutch physicist who became Professor of Experimental Physics at Leyden where he founded the Cryogenic Laboratory in 1894. He discovered the principle of superconductivity and received the Nobel Prize for Physics in 1913.

PETER KAPITZA (1894–   )
Russian scientist who left his home country in 1921 and later returned in 1934. Kapitza discovered new methods of liquefying hydrogen and helium that could be used industrially. In 1938 he conducted brilliant experiments into the properties of liquid helium. He researched the atomic and hydrogen bomb projects for the U.S.S.R.

JACOB PERKINS and JAMES HARRISON
In 1834, Perkins — an American living in Britain — patented his design for a refrigerator which produced cold by evaporating volatile fluids. Perkins did not develop his invention. Possibly independently of Perkins, a Scot called Harrison, living in Australia, designed a refrigerator. Harrison's designs were used by Siebe to produce the first commercial refrigerator in 1862.

KELVIN, LORD (1824–1907)
Kelvin did much to establish the theory and practice of thermodynamics. He was the first to suggest an Absolute Zero temperature and his name has been given to the Absolute or Kelvin scale of temperature. This scale is used by scientists in the field of cryogenics, a science dedicated to the study of very low temperatures. The word is made up from two words — *kruos*, which is Greek for 'very cold' and *genes* which is a Latin word for 'producing'. Roughly speaking, cryogenic studies begin at around −185°C (−301°F) but really interesting changes in the behaviour of substances begin at −230°C (−382°F).

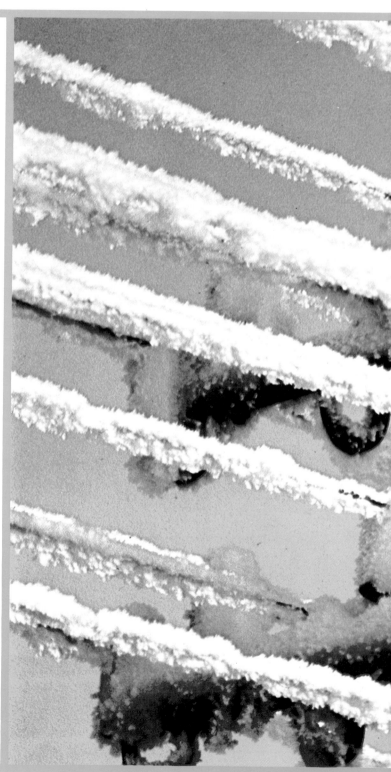

TEMPERATURE SCALES

Centigrade and Fahrenheit are the two most common scales for measuring temperature. Our chart indicates the difference between the two. You can do your own conversions by following these rules. To convert Centigrade to Fahrenheit divide by five and multiply by nine, then add 32. If the Centigrade figure is a minus figure, divide by five and multiply by nine and subtract 32. To convert Fahrenheit to Centigrade subtract 32, divide by nine and multiply by five. However, if it is a minus figure add 32 and divide by nine and multiply by five. Here are some practical examples of how to convert these temperatures.

CENTIGRADE (+) to FAHRENHEIT

$$275°C \div 5 = 55 \times 9 = 495 + 32 = 527°F$$

CENTIGRADE (−) TO FAHRENHEIT

$$-85°C \div 5 = 17 \times 9 = 153 - 32 = -121°F$$

FAHRENHEIT (+) TO CENTIGRADE

$$356°F - 32 = 324 \div 9 = 36 \times 5 = 180°C$$

FAHRENHEIT (−) TO CENTIGRADE

$$-310°F + 32 = 342 \div 9 = 38 \times 5 = 190°C$$

THE AUTHOR

Michal Kentzer was born in 1945. He was educated at the Sheffield City College of Education and Sheffield University where he gained a General Honours degree in Botany and Zoology. Since 1968 he has taught in a variety of Grammar, Comprehensive and Junior Schools, and is now Deputy Headmaster of a Middle School in charge of Environmental Studies. He has contributed articles to periodicals and newspapers.

1 2 3 4 5 6 7 8 9 10—CAD—85 84 83 82 81 80 79